JUDE
2 PETER

ABINGDON NEW TESTAMENT COMMENTARIES

JUDE
2 PETER

STEVEN J. KRAFTCHICK

Abingdon Press
Nashville

ABINGDON NEW TESTAMENT COMMENTARIES:
JUDE, 2 PETER

This book is printed on recycled, acid-free, elemental-chlorine–free paper.

Library of Congress Cataloging-in-Publication Data

Kraftchick, Steven John.
   Jude, 2 Peter / Steven J. Kraftchick.
      p. cm.—(Abingdon New Testament commentaries)
Includes bibliographical references and index.
   ISBN 0-687-05762-0 (pbk.: alk. paper)
   1. Bible. N.T. Jude—Commentaries. 2. Bible. N.T. 2
Peter—Commentaries. I. Title: Jude, two Peter. II. Title: Jude, Second
Peter. III. Title. IV. Series.
   BS2815.3 .K73 2002
   227'.9307—dc21

                        2002006057

02 03 04 05 06 07 08 09 10 11—10 9 8 7 6 5 4 3 2 1

MANUFACTURED IN THE UNITED STATES OF AMERICA

CONTENTS

FOREWORD

The *Abingdon New Testament Commentaries* series provides compact, critical commentaries on the writings of the New Testament. These commentaries are written with special attention to the needs and interests of theological students, but they will also be useful for students in upper-level college or university settings, as well as for pastors and other church leaders. In addition to providing basic information about the New Testament texts and insights into their meanings, these commentaries are intended to exemplify the tasks and procedures of careful, critical biblical exegesis.

The authors who have contributed to this series come from a wide range of ecclesiastical affiliations and confessional stances. All are seasoned, respected scholars and experienced classroom teachers. They take full account of the most important current scholarship and secondary literature, but do not attempt to summarize that literature or engage in technical academic debate. Their fundamental concern is to analyze the literary, socio-historical, theological, and ethical dimensions of the biblical texts themselves. Although all of the commentaries in this series have been written on the basis of the Greek texts, the authors do not presuppose any knowledge of the biblical languages on the part of the reader. When some awareness of the grammatical, syntactical, or philological issue is necessary for an adequate understanding of a particular text, they explain the matter clearly and concisely.

The introduction of each volume ordinarily includes subdivisions dealing with the *key issues* addressed and/or raised by the New Testament writing under consideration; its *literary genre, structure, and character;* its *occasion and situational context,* including its wider social, historical, and religious contexts; and its *theological and ethical significance* within these several contexts.

In each volume, the *commentary* is organized according to literary units rather than verse by verse. Generally, each of these units is the subject of three types of analysis. First, the *literary analysis* attends to the unit's genre, most important stylistic features, and overall structure. Second, the *exegetical analysis* considers the aim and leading ideas of the unit, deals with any especially important textual variants, and discusses the meanings of important words, phrases, and images. It also takes note of the particular historical and social situations of the writer and original readers, and of the wider cultural and religious contexts of the book as a whole. Finally, the *theological and ethical analysis* discusses the theological and ethical matters with which the unit deals or to which it points, focusing on the theological and ethical significance of the text within its original setting.

Each volume also includes a *select bibliography,* thereby providing guidance to other major commentaries and important scholarly works, and a brief *subject index.* The New Revised Standard Version of the Bible is the principal translation of reference for the series, but the authors draw on all of the major modern English versions, and when necessary provide their own original translations of difficult terms or phrases.

The fundamental aim of this series will have been attained if readers are assisted, not only to understand more about the origins, character, and meaning of the New Testament writings, but also to enter into their own informed and critical engagement with the texts themselves.

Victor Paul Furnish
General Editor

PREFACE

My initial readings of Jude and 2 Peter, like those of many readers, were disquieting. The tone of these letters, along with their seemingly intractable insistence on distinguishing "insiders" from "outsiders"—between *us* and *them*—makes an indelible impression. Eventually, I came to appreciate these letters—and their writers—for their commitments and for their efforts to engage honestly the fundamental elements of Christianity. That is not to say that I read them now with any less discomfort, but the reasons for my discomfort are now quite different from those that initially affected me.

Since 2 Peter uses Jude as a source, it is understandable that the two letters are often read in tandem. However, this has the unfortunate side effect of diminishing the very real differences between them. To appreciate Jude and 2 Peter fully, they should be read individually, and each letter's argument should be given its due. I have tried to do this in the commentary and I hope that readers will benefit from it. The two writers make equally significant, but distinctly different, efforts to translate Christian faith into the vernacular of their audiences while maintaining the commitments that faith entails. Anyone who has attempted to do this knows how difficult it is, and Jude and 2 Peter can be valuable guides for that necessary task.

In the aftermath of the tragic events in Washington, D.C. and New York City on September 11, 2001, many people have discussed the roles that religion sometimes plays in creating boundaries between peoples and promulgating acts of violence. Second Peter and Jude speak of such boundaries and of the judgment that comes on those who violate them. However, it is also clear that both documents reserve the prerogative of judgment for God alone. Read in the context of nascent communities that were trying to survive, such rhetoric has one meaning. Read outside of that context, these texts can be used for harm. It is my hope that this commentary will help readers understand the rhetoric of these letters in their proper contexts.

Readers will readily note my indebtedness to the commentaries of Richard Bauckham and J. N. D. Kelly. Read side by side, they illumine the issues of these letters and clarify the interpreter's tasks.

The infelicities and errors are mine, but those comments that are of some value are the result of many peoples' efforts. I am grateful to them all. To Rex Matthews for inviting me to participate in the series, to Diane Springfield without whose efforts on my behalf this text could not have been written, to Jack Elliott for his sustained efforts as my editor, to Victor Furnish for his direction at particularly critical moments, and to Karoline Lewis for her help in reading early drafts, my deepest thanks. I am especially grateful to Bryan Whitfield for his keen ability to whittle and refine my prose and make it clearer and more precise. I am also grateful for the support of friends and colleagues at the Candler School of Theology.

I dedicate the volume to C. A., who spent more than enough time waiting for "Jude the obscure" to come to an end. Thank you all.

Steven J. Kraftchick

LIST OF ABBREVIATIONS

1 [2] Clem.	*First [Second] Clement*
1 Enoch	*1 Enoch* (Ethiopic Apocalypse)
1QHª	*Hodayot*ª or *Thanksgiving Hymns*ª
1 QM	*Milḥamah* or *War Scroll*
1QS	*Rule of the Community* (Qumran Cave 1)
2 Apoc. Bar.	*Syriac Apocalypse of Baruch*
3 Macc.	*3 Maccabees*
AB	Anchor Bible
ABD	*Anchor Bible Dictionary*, D. N. Freedman (ed.)
ACNT	Augsburg Commentaries on the New Testament
Abr.	Philo, *On the Life of Abraham*
Acts Pet.	*Acts of Peter*
Adv. Haer.	Irenaeus, *Against Heresies*
AnBib	Analecta biblica
ANRW	*Aufstieg und Niedergang der römischen Welt*
Ant.	Josephus, *Jewish Antiquities*
ANTC	Abingdon New Testament Commentaries
AT	Author's Translation
BDAG	Bauer W., F. W. Danker, W. F. Arndt, and F. W. Gingrich. *Greek-English Lexicon of the New Testament and other Early Christian Literature*. 3d ed. Chicago, 1999
Barn.	*Barnabas*
Bib	*Biblica*
BSac	*Bibilotheca sacra*
CBQ	*Catholic Biblical Quarterly*

CD	Cairo Genizah copy of the *Damascus Document*
ConBNT	Coniectanea biblica New Testament Series
CNT	Commentaire du Nouveau Testament
CTJ	*Calvin Theological Journal*
De Color	Aristotle, *Colors*
Dial. Trypho	Justin Martyr, *Dialogue with Trypho*
Did.	*Didache*
Diog. Laert.	Diogenes Laertius
Ebr.	Philo, *On Drunkenness*
EKKNT	Evangelisch-katholischer Kommentar zum Neuen Testament
Epic.	*Epictetus*
EvQ	*Evangelical Quarterly*
Gos. Pet.	*Gospel of Peter*
Herm. Man.	*Hermas, Mandate (s)*
Herm. Vis.	*Hermas, Visions (s)*
Hist. Eccl.	Eusebius, *The History of the Church*
HNT	Handbuch zum Neuen Testament
HNTC	Harper's New Testament Commentaries
HTKNT	Herders theologischer Kommentar zum Neuen Testament
HTR	*Harvard Theological Review*
IBC	Interpretation: A Bible Commentary for Teaching and Preaching
ICC	International Critical Commentary
IDB	*Interpreter's Dictionary of the Bible,* G. A. Buttrick (ed.)
IDBSup	*Interpreter's Dictionary of the Bible: Supplementary Volume*
JB	The Jerusalem Bible
JBL	*Journal of Biblical Literature*
JSNT	*Journal for the Study of the New Testament*
JSNTSup	Journal for the Study of the New Testament: Supplement Series
JSOT	*Journal for the Study of the Old Testament*
JSOTSup	Journal for the Study of the Old Testament: Supplement Series

Jub.	*Jubilees*
J. W.	Josephus, *Jewish War*
KJV	King James Version
LSJ	Liddell Scott Jones, *A Greek-English Lexicon*
LXX	Septuagint
Mart. Pol.	*Martyrdom of Polycarp*
MeyerK	H. A. W. Meyer, Kritisch-exegetischer Kommentar über das Neue Testament
Midr. Ps.	*Midrash* on the Psalms
Migration	Philo, *On the Migration of Abraham*
Mos.	Philo, *On the Life of Moses*
Mor.	Plutarch, *Moralia*
MT	Masoretic Text
Mut.	Philo, *On the Change of Names*
Nat. Deor.	Cicero, *On the Nature of the Gods*
NCB	New Century Bible
NEB	The New English Bible
NICNT	New International Commentary on the New Testament
NIV	New International Version
NovT	*Novum Testamentum*
NRSV	New Revised Standard Version
NTS	*New Testament Studies*
OTP	*The Old Testament Pseudepigrapha*, James H. Charlesworth (ed.)
Pass. Perp. Fel.	Martydom of Perpetua and Felicity
Pol. *Phil.*	Polycarp, *Letter to the Philippians*
RB	*Revue biblique*
REB	The Revised English Bible
RSV	Revised Standard Version
SBLDS	Society of Biblical Literature Dissertation Series
SBLMS	Society of Biblical Literature Monograph Series
Sanh.	*Sanhedrin*
SecCent	*Second Century*
Sir.	Sirach/Ecclesiasticus

Syb. Or.	*Sibylline Oracles*
T. Ash.	*Testament of Asher*
T. Benj.	*Testament of Benjamin*
T. Jud.	*Testament of Judah*
T. Levi	*Testament of Levi*
TDNT	*Theological Dictionary of the New Testament*, G. Kittel and G. Friedrich (eds.)
TNTC	Tyndale New Testament Commentaries
TS	*Theological Studies*
TynBul	*Tyndale Bulletin*
VC	*Vigliae christianae*
Vit. Cypr.	*Life of Cyprian*
WBC	Word Biblical Commentary
Wis	Wisdom of Solomon
WUNT	Wissenschaftliche Untersuchungen zum Neuen Testament
Yoma	Yoma (=Kippurim)
ZNW	*Zeitschrift für die neutestamentliche Wissenschaft*

INTRODUCTION: JUDE

This short letter is not read often or studied much, and while this is understandable, Jude deserves more than the "benign neglect" which has been its lot (Elliott 1982, 161). Admittedly, there are good reasons for the neglect. The letter is filled with strange language and obscure references (e.g., vv. 5, 11), it is polemical and uncompromising, and its author appears to satirize and disparage his opponents rather than engaging their thought and teaching (e.g., vv. 12-13). Moreover, the author's own thoughts are embedded in his polemic and even a sympathetic reader must work hard at uncovering them. Hence, it is not a surprise that Jude has never enjoyed a high rank in the New Testament canon.

Yet, despite these traits, there are equally good reasons to include Jude as part of the Church's self-reflections. First, the letter is a warning against self-delusion, something with which the Church has always struggled. Jude reminds the Church that its chosen status is not only a privilege, but also entails a responsibility. Second, because its author recognizes how narrow the difference is between faithfulness and infidelity, Jude calls the Church to a life of self-scrutiny. Finally, Jude reminds its readers that a life of fidelity requires both the diligent pursuit of truth and obedience to it (see vv. 5-7, 17-18).

GENRE, CHARACTER, AND OCCASION

In many aspects Jude is an anomaly. It is a letter "never intended" but eventually considered essential by its author (v. 3). It is indebted to Jewish apocalyptic ideas and morality (vv. 5-7,

9, 14-15), but addresses a Gentile audience. It employs ancient literary and oratorical forms, but is not bound to them. It insists on fidelity to the past, but its author modifies scriptural traditions and authoritative witnesses to achieve his own argumentative designs.

Jude begins with a conventional salutation and a wish for "peace" (vv. 1-2), which are followed by the letter's themes (vv. 3-4): contending for the truth in thought and action. Although the author initially desired to write about "our common salvation" (v. 3), he felt compelled to change course because a dangerous group of teachers had infiltrated the church. He therefore begins his "contention for the faith" (v. 3) by warning his audience about those who "deny the authority of God and Christ" (v. 4). To develop these themes, the author has replaced the typical body of a letter with an extended reinterpretation of scriptural references and texts (vv. 5-19). These create a cohesive argument about the nature of disobedience (vv. 5-7, 11) and the future judgment of those who persist in it (vv. 14-15, 17-18). The author applies to his own situation a series of examples drawn from ancient authorities (vv. 8, 10, 12-13) and identifies his opponents as "ungodly sinners," whom the authorities had predicted (vv. 14-16, 19). He concludes by exhorting the audience to persist in faithfulness (vv. 20-23) and by offering a doxology (vv. 24-25). Because Jude does not follow ancient epistolary conventions, some commentators have argued that it is a fictional letter. However, the author's urgent tone (v. 3) and the specificity of his exhortations and warnings (vv. 17-23) suggest that Jude is a genuine letter written to combat false teaching (see Bauckham 1990, 150; Watson 1988, 29-30).

Four stylistic devices integrate the argument: comparison and contrast, a calculated use of hyperbole, poetic chaining through repetition, and the use of triads and catchwords. Throughout the letter the opposition is compared to ancient examples of disobedience and unbelief (vv. 8-10, 12-13, 16, 19) and contrasted to the "beloved" members of Jude's audience (vv. 17, 20). The dramatic hyperbole Jude uses further establishes how serious the matters at hand really are. The other teachers are not simply present; they are "intruders" (v. 4). They do not just hold another viewpoint, they are ignorant (v. 10) and "deny the master" (v. 4). Moreover, their faulty thinking has turned them into people who "defile the flesh" (v. 8), "revile what they do not understand" (v. 10), and who "follow their own ungodly desires" (vv. 15, 16, 18).

There are at least twenty sets of triads in this brief letter (Charles 1990, 124, n.60). These range from the author's initial self-identification as "Jude, servant of Jesus Christ, and brother of James" (v. 1), to the final doxology, which lauds the one who is "before all time, now, and forever." The main argument is constructed from two sets of three examples of disobedience: verses 5-7 and verse 11. The author also employs a triple description when he notes his opponents' moral lapses (vv. 12-13). The triple formulations underscore the urgency of the letter, attempting to make the readers see and feel the magnitude of the danger in their midst. Their use lends depth and vividness to the author's argument, causing his positive statements about God and the community to stand in direct contrast with the negative portrait of the antagonists.

Jude uses catchwords; e.g., "ungodly/ungodliness" (vv. 4, 15, 18), "kept" (vv. 1, 6, 13, 21, 24), "saints/holy" (vv. 3, 14, 20, 24), and "love/beloved" (vv. 1, 2, 12, 17, 20, 21), to knit the letter's various parts into a cohesive whole. By repeating the terms "love/beloved" the author creates an *inclusio* between the opening admonition—to contend for the faith (v. 3)—and the exhortations that close the letter (vv. 20-23). By his use of "these/these people" (vv. 8, 10, 11, 12, 14, 16, 19), his initial charges against the opposition as "intruders" and rebels who deny the Master and Lord (v. 4) are connected with the examples of disobedience set forth in vv. 5-19.

Because of the author's terse and oblique manner of referring to the oppositions' teaching, and the fact that he attributes only illegitimate and selfish motives for their actions and beliefs, we can only hazard very general comments about the opponents.

First, it is important to recognize that they would not have considered themselves as opponents of the faith, but as teachers who were enhancing it (vv. 11-13). They understood themselves as

Spirit-driven people (v. 19) who, based on revelatory dreams (v. 8), taught that the freedom created by God's grace was absolute and therefore released true believers from the social constraints of morality (vv. 10, 18, 19). In some manner, they would have considered their teaching as an extension of the Church's belief in the universal and all-inclusive scope of God's grace. They may have resembled those addressed by Paul who misunderstood God's grace as a license to sin and who thought that eschatological existence in Christ ended all need for obedience to the norms of social morality (see Rom 6:1; 1 Cor 5:1-2, 12).

The author disputes their claims to inspiration and spiritual maturity (v. 19), claiming that the opponents were not wise but ignorant, which resulted in their arrogant disregard for tradition and authority (vv. 4, 8, 10). Moreover, he argues that their claims to freedom misappropriated the grace of God and were only excuses to indulge in their own immoral desires (v. 16). Thus, rather than strengthening the community with their teaching, they were dividing it. Therefore, Jude wrote as an intervention, addressing the emergency created by these teachers who were confusing believers with an injurious message of false freedom (vv. 4, 10, 16, 19). The author feared that his audience did not perceive the danger these intruders posed. To alert them and to reveal the teachers' actual nature, Jude engages in "rhetorical outrage" (Johnson 1999, 498), writing a letter filled with dramatic contrasts, devastating consequences, and condemnation rather than an essay of even-handed demonstration or a logical debate. He appeals to his hearers' emotions as well as their minds. Only by engaging them at this level can he hope to succeed in his warnings.

AUTHOR AND DATE OF COMPOSITION

The author calls himself "Jude, the brother of James" (v. 1). Most likely the "James" referred to is the "Lord's brother" (Mark 6:3), who was a leader of the Jerusalem church (see Acts 15; Gal 1:19, 2:9). Some commentators argue that this Jude was the actual author of the letter (Bauckham 1983, 15). However, the author's command of literary Greek, a trait more likely to be found among Hellenistic Jews than among those of Palestinian origin, weighs against this. Thus, while it cannot be ruled out entirely, it is unlikely that Jude, the brother of James and Jesus, authored this letter.

We know little about this Jude or his activities, and why the author chose this pseudonym is not self-evident. At best, we can suggest that he chose the name because of Jude's connection with the early leaders of the Church and the authority that would have implied.

The call "to remember the apostolic predictions" in verse 17 has been used as a key for the dating of the epistle. Scholars disagree about what Jude meant with the phrase "by the apostles." Some consider this a reference to specific missionaries (either one of the initial apostles or those later designated as apostles) who had preached to the audience (Bauckham 1983, 103). Others take the term in a collective sense and think that Jude was referring not to any specific apostles but to all those known by that title (Kelly 1981, 281). They thus suggest that the term had a technical sense like "the prophets" or "the ancestors" which would not have occurred until late in the first century.

Probably Jude did use the term with a collective sense, but this does not imply that the letter was written at the very end of the first century. The call to "remember the predictions of the apostles" suggests only that his audience was familiar with early Christian eschatological tradition. It says nothing about when these predictions were made. As a result, the verse proves neither that the apostolic age has passed (Kelly 1981, 281) nor that there were readers of the letter who were converted directly by some apostles (Bauckham 1983, 104). Jude simply states that the readers were taught that "scoffers" would come in the future during the end time. Thus, despite initial appearances, the phrases in verses 17 and 18 do not provide a basis for an early dating of the letter or a very late one.

The problems addressed in the letter—the appearance of false teachers and the clarification of the church's moral boundaries—

were typical concerns of the early Gentile church. Hence the letter might be dated anywhere from 50–100 CE. Since it is likely that Jude was a source for 2 Peter (see Introduction to 2 Peter), an upper limit would be somewhere before 100 CE. The references to the early Church's received faith (v. 3) and to the apostles as a corporate authority (v. 17) suggest a date between 75–100 CE.

THEOLOGY AND ETHICS

In such a short letter, written as a warning, one cannot expect a fully developed theology. In fact, the author's comments indicate that his letter was not intended for theological reflection, but as an intervention to protect the "common salvation." Theology for him is not *de novo*, but an enterprise of building upon the received traditions (vv. 20). Hence he employed a strategy of retrieval, using the past in order to clarify the present. Because he wished to reveal the error of the intruders, especially their arrogant disrespect for God (vv. 4, 5, 6, 7, 10, 11, 15), his goal was not to write a theological essay, but to draw out theological implications, especially the ethics of belief.

Jude emphasizes God's holy nature, but this is done indirectly through references to God's initiatives toward and for human beings: establishing the believing community as holy (vv. 3, 20), executing judgment on the disobedient (vv. 5, 15), and preserving the unblemished ones for glory (v. 24). God's holiness also is implied by repeated references to "ungodliness" (vv. 4, 15, 18) that are contrasted with the steadfast nature of God which demands reverence and awe (vv. 9, 23). Thus while the ungodly "pervert God's grace, turning it into licentiousness" (v. 4), and act and speak in rebellion (v. 15), God delivers humans from bondage and peril (v. 6), loves the believers steadfastly (vv. 1, 21), and protects the beloved community (vv. 1, 21, 24-25).

Given his interest in exposing the nature of ungodliness, it is interesting that the author provides no specific descriptions of sin, other than its relationship to disobedience. The author does not concern himself with initial states of sin or distance from

God, but concentrates on the life required of those who have accepted God's work through Christ. As a result, purity and fidelity become matters of remaining in the grace of God, rather than individual traits or behaviors.

While God remains his primary focus, the author does attribute to Christ significant and powerful functions typically associated with God. For example, the term *kyrios* ("Lord") is used seven times in the letter. In four instances, *kyrios* is directly applied to Jesus Christ (vv. 4, 17, 21, 25), and in two others a connection is implied (vv. 5, 14). In this regard, Jude displays a tendency found in other early Christian writing, namely, the transfer of titles, traditionally reserved for Yahweh, to Christ as the agent of God. Nevertheless, Jude still understood Jesus as *God's* Christ and the "christology" of the letter is not developed independently of that fact (vv. 1, 4, 17, 21, 25).

The letter connects Christ to God primarily in reference to Christ's eschatological function. The author believed that he lived at the end of time and the eschatological appearance of Christ dominates his thought. Holy believers are kept for the appearance of Christ (vv. 1, 21, 25). Through Christ, God has established sovereignty (v. 4), and by him will execute eschatological judgment (v. 15). Salvation will occur in Christ (v. 1), but only as an eschatological reality (v. 21), guaranteed by obedience. The proper response to the eschatological Lord is obedience, which the author understands as the natural response of trust. Accepting this, it is through Christ that the church expresses its praise and glorification of God (v. 25) while it awaits the Lord's return.

Jude is not an epistle one reads for comfort or to ponder esoteric questions about theology; it is a letter of challenge. It is a letter of outrage, and we are unaccustomed to this much passion. The letter's uncompromising insistence that faith is an ethical entity forces its readers into critical self-examination and causes us to examine our habits of self-deception. Jude calls the readers to the responsibility of their beliefs, and one reads it not to hear about "release of the captives," but to learn of the responsibilities of being released.

COMMENTARY: JUDE

PRESCRIPT (1-2)

The letter begins with two typical ancient epistolary conventions: an opening by which the author identifies himself and his recipients, followed by a greeting.

◊ ◊ ◊ ◊

The author introduces himself as Jude, a *doulos* ("servant") of Christ. It is probable that he was using a pseudonym (see Introduction). The name he has chosen was common in the ancient world, so he specifies his identity as a "servant of Christ" and the "brother of James." "Servant of the Lord" often designated those whom God chose for leadership or specific tasks (e.g., Moses, Neh 9:14; Abraham, Ps 105:42; David, Ps 89:3). Jude has adopted the term to indicate that God had called him into the service of Christ, and his letter should be understood as an instance of his obedience to that call.

"Jude's" status may have been no more authoritative than that of the teachers he calls "intruders." If so, his self-identification as a "servant of Christ" is an attempt to establish his authority with the audience (see Rom 1:1; Gal 1:10; Phil 1:1). As a "servant of Christ," Jude implies that Christ has designated him to act as his representative. The self-identification also contrasts with that of his opponents who "deny our only master and Lord Jesus Christ" (v. 4). Jude thus establishes his God-granted authority to speak for the faith, his own fidelity to Christ, and implicitly questions the validity of the intruders' interpretations of the gospel. In effect, this simple designation begins the process by which Jude will challenge their character and teaching.

Jude also refers to himself as "the brother of James." There are a number of people named "James" in the New Testament including James the son of Alphaeus (Mark 3:18), and James the son of Zebedee (Mark 1:19). The only likely candidate is "James, the brother of the Lord" (Gal 1:19). This James was the only one the early church consistently called "James," and Jude is named specifically as the brother of James and Jesus in Mark 6:3 and Matt 13:54.

According to tradition, James was an influential interpreter of the faith from the earliest days of the Church's existence. As an eyewitness of the resurrected Jesus (1 Cor 15:7), and as one of the prime developers of the Church's corporate ethical responsibilities (Acts 15:13-21; 21:18, 25), any teaching gleaned from James would have found wide acceptance. As his brother, Jude is identified with a leading authority of the foundational church; a status the opposition cannot claim.

Jude's decision to call himself "the brother of James" rather than the "brother of Jesus" is perplexing. If the author expected his relationship to James to supply force for his claims, then calling himself "brother of Jesus" could only do so to a greater degree. Why did he not simply use the term "brother of the Lord"? An answer is not easily provided. Perhaps it was a matter of deference, since " 'Brother of the Lord' was not an official designation, and, if used by Jude himself, might seem to imply a claim to an authority above that of an apostle" (Bigg 1961, 319). It is more likely, however, that the title "brother of the Lord" combined with the opening phrase "slave of Jesus Christ" would have been incongruous, a semantic anomaly (Bauckham 1983, 25). Further reference to the human filial relationship might have suggested that the author did not show proper deference to Jesus' status as the Christ.

The specificity of Jude's self-identification does not carry over to the addressees. Epistolary conventions typically included geographic information about the audience, but Jude instead identifies the audience using only religious language. He replaces the identification of geographical location with a reference to God's love ("those who are called, who are beloved in God"), and the standard calendar date gives way to the transhistorical moment of Christ's second coming, which is above and beyond calendrical, historical measurement. Jude repeats the language of the opening phrases in verse 21 so that at both the beginning and the conclusion of the letter, he reinforces the relationship of the audience to God's love and care through Christ.

It is critical to Jude's argument that the addressees recognize themselves as "called people," created by God's love expressed in Christ. Since God has called the community into existence, it must rely upon God for its continued existence, both in the present and for the future. Even though Christian proclamation gave it a particular hue, the concept of "God's called people" has its roots in ancient Israel. Israel was chosen by God through divine initiative to serve God's purposes for the world. The call of Israel involves God's promise to strengthen and protect the people, but required a response of allegiance to God's covenant (Isa 42:6-7). The "call" is not one of right, but conferral of privilege. Jude uses the language of "call" not only to affirm the congregation's security, but also to remind them of their responsibility.

As Jude will show (vv. 5-16), failure to live according to the responsibility of the call results in a loss of this privileged status. These themes of fidelity and responsibility recur throughout the letter, as does the fact that the status can be forfeited by disobedience. These ideas are the basis for his refutation of the opposition (vv. 4-16) and the foundation of his exhortations (vv. 17-22).

Jude modifies the identification "called ones" with two participial phrases, "beloved in God the Father" and "kept safe for Jesus Christ." The passive forms of the participles imply *divine* action and the fact that the called ones have done nothing to merit their favored condition. God's graciousness conveys it and God's divine power maintains it. "To be called" is to be redeemed by God through the event of Christ (see 1 Cor 1:2) and thus to be "loved by him" (see Rom 5:8). The participle "beloved" has a perfect tense: God's loving actions, once having begun, remain constant. God will not retract favor unless the recipients refuse it.

Jude uses the noun "beloved" or a cognate form when he addresses the readers (vv. 1, 2, 3, 17, 20, 21). This description distinguishes them from Jude's opponents who are "ungodly persons, who pervert the grace of God," and who are "designated for judgment" (v. 3). In this verse, the verb "kept" indicates God's eschatological protection of believers. Elsewhere, the author uses the same term for affirming the effect and extent of God's power for punishment (v. 6), maintaining a proper relationship with God (v. 6), and for the eternal protection shown to God's followers (v. 24).

God's love also involves God's protection: the believers are "kept safe," i.e., established by God and maintained for the second coming when the ultimate consummation will occur (v. 24). At the beginning of the letter (v. 1) and at its end (vv. 21, 24), the author establishes this eschatological perspective. The promise of "being kept by God" underlines the certainty that God's will is to sustain and protect them from harm.

New Testament letters typically include an opening wish for "grace and peace" (e.g., Rom 1:7; 1 Cor 1:3; Gal 1:3; Phil 1:2; 2 Peter 1:2). In verse 2, Jude offers a similar wish, but his triadic formulation is unique. First and 2 Timothy also use a triple greeting ("grace, mercy, peace," 1 Tim 1:2; 2 Tim 1:2) but Jude alone uses "mercy, peace, and love." Ancient Jewish letter writers used the phrase "mercy and peace" to express their desire that the divine blessings of *hesed* and *shalom* rest on the letter's recipients always and everywhere. Jude's formulation "May mercy, peace, and love be yours in abundance" bears a close resemblance to these Jewish blessings, but it adds the term "love" to their typical dyad. This addition provides Christian overtones to the wish and emphasizes a fundamental theme (vv. 1, 2, 3, 17, 20, 21), "the love of God," as a foundation for God's community. The blessing also signals other important themes of the letter. The readers must show mercy to others, since they enjoy it themselves (vv. 22-23). They must be vigilant about the church's wellbeing, especially since there are some who wish to destroy it by causing division (vv. 19-20). Finally, and in contrast to the opposition, who care only for their own gain (v. 16), the congregation must remain attentive to its members, keeping themselves in the love of God (v. 21; so Neyrey 1993, 46).

THEMATIC STATEMENT (3-4)

By their placement and content, these verses are the most important statements for interpreting the letter. In them the author expresses the goal and strategy of his argument. Jude had a two-fold purpose: (1) to warn the community of the invasive and dangerous teachers whose presence threatens its existence, and (2) to strengthen the community so that it can resist the intruders and retain their divinely-ordained condition of redemption.

Linguistic and conceptual links between these verses and the rest of the letter reflect their dual purpose. The readers are addressed as "beloved" in verse 3 and verses 17, 20; see also 21. The terms "faith" (v. 20), "salvation/save" (v. 23), and "holiness" (v. 20) all echo the concern that the community of saints "contend for the faith." Jude connects verse 4 to verses 5-19 by the repetition of the terms "judgment" (vv. 6, 9, 15) and "ungodly" (vv. 15, 18). References to immorality (vv. 6, 7, 8, 12, 16, 18) and to the denial of proper authority (vv. 5, 6, 8, 9, 16, 18, 19) also underscore the connection. Thus, from the outset, Jude displays two goals: to expose the false teachers and to exhort the believers to a life of faith.

The author begins his own "contention" for the faith by displaying the fate of those who transgressed their relationship with God, i.e., those who did not respond with obedience to the status divinely granted to them (vv. 4b-19). Once he has underscored the serious nature of maintaining a covenant with God, the author then encourages his readers to exhibit mutual edification, to pray, to act from love, and to maintain a stance of hope (vv. 20-21). This is behavior he considers contending for the faith, for by these actions the faithful community is preserved for eternal glory (v. 24).

◊   ◊   ◊   ◊

Verse 3 suggests that the present letter was not what the author originally intended to write. Initially intending to write about "their shared salvation," he realized that a letter of another sort must be drafted first. How he came to this realization is not clear. The phrase "I found it necessary" sounds a note of urgency and importance; other issues had to be postponed to deal with the emergency. Verse 4 reveals the stimulus for his change of course: the appearance of "intruders" who "deny our only Master and Lord" by "perverting" God's grace. It is doubtful that the audience recognized these people as intruders or as dangerous, and the letter was written to alert them to these realities.

So, in place of remarks on "our common salvation," Jude appeals to his readers to "continue to contend for the faith." In its cultural context, the term "to contend" referred to athletic contests, but philosophical and religious thinkers also used it to depict life as a moral contest. This metaphor emphasizes that the congregation must see the "intruders" as opponents to the gospel, and, unless the members act with skill, endurance, and savvy, their opponents will overcome them (see 2 Cor 10:3-6). The early church was a fragile institution, dependent on the confession of an extraordinary and unusual narrative. "Contending for the faith" entails maintaining fidelity to the founding narrative: clarifying it and acting upon it (v. 20). It involves both a defense against false or faulty understandings of the gospel (Gal 1:8-9, 2:14) and efforts to maintain the social fabric of the community (Rom 12:1-13).

The congregation is to contend for "the faith that was once and for all entrusted to the saints." The term *hapax* ("once for all") does not mean a calcified or rigid construction of doctrine, but a narrative of faith that is complete. The term is used here, as it is in Heb 9:12, 26-28 and in 1 Pet 3:18, to mean that God's saving actions in Christ are sufficient and final, in need of no additional efforts or repetition. The narrative of those acts delivered to the community contains everything necessary for a life of faith and recounts truthfully everything required for salvation. Jude uses "once for all" to underscore that the instruction the audience initially accepted is a sufficient and complete narration of the gospel message.

This "faith entrusted to the saints" concerns the common salvation to which Jude has just referred. It is "the message or body of saving beliefs accepted as orthodox in the Church" (Kelly 1981, 247), so when the author uses the term *pistis* ("faith") to signify a body of belief, he is not at odds with other New Testament writers (e.g., Paul uses *pistis* to describe his early preaching [Gal 1:23, Rom 10:8], and Luke refers to the gospel message as "the faith" [Acts 6:7]).

"Entrusted" is a technical term, taken over from Judaism, referring to an authoritative chain of tradition that guarantees the truth of the teaching passed down from one generation to the next. Thus Jude was emphasizing the legitimate nature and true content of the faith. It is clear that the authoritative transmission of "the faith" also was important to other New Testament writers (e.g., Luke 1:1-4), for, like Jude, they refer to a transmission of fundamental traditions (1 Cor 11:2, 23; 2 Thess 2:15, 3:6) and frequently make use of them (1 Cor 11:23, Phil 2:5-11, 1 Tim 3:16, 2 Tim 2:11-13). In all these cases, they reflect a movement toward refining the faith and providing guarantees of its authenticity.

In verse 4, Jude describes the opposition. Most certainly they considered themselves believers. Jude, however, never refers to them that way, but only as "those who have stolen in among you" or simply as "those" or "they" (vv.8, 10, 11, 12, 14). Jude does not mean that the opposition has physically entered the congregation by stealth, but that they have entered the community's life like viruses that infect a body, which, if left untreated, will eventually kill their hosts. The intruders' teaching, seemingly innocuous, is actually a hidden danger, which God has already condemned (v. 4*b*). Jude aims to make their real identity apparent, and the fact that his readers were oblivious to the danger created by intruders explains the letter's harsh tone.

Elsewhere Jude refers to the opposing intruders as "these people" (vv. 8, 10, 11, 12, 14), suggesting that they merit neither a name nor a mention of what they actually taught. Indeed, the author never engages the intruders' teaching directly. Instead, he employs arguments against their character and behavior, exposing them as disingenuous and hypocritical. While Jude and the addressees are "obedient and loved by God" (v. 1), the opposition perverts "grace into licentiousness" and denies "divine lordship." While these phrases are stereotypical, and likely are exaggerated, the charges contained some truth, since otherwise the audience would not have accepted them. Thus, the innovators probably promoted some form of liberty from external constraints, including those that pertained to social and personal behavior.

Jude claims that the innovators "long ago were designated (in writing) for this condemnation as ungodly." Although the adverb "long ago" can simply mean an event that occurred "prior to this time" (e.g., 2 Cor 12:19), it typically suggests that the object under consideration was long held or established (e.g., Heb 1:1). This meaning fits Jude's context: from the very beginning, well before they entered this community, these teachers were designated for condemnation.

Although the author's general meaning is clear, the phrase as a whole poses significant difficulties. What did Jude intend by "this condemnation," and to what source was he referring when he stated that it had been "already designated"? Commentators have suggested sources such as the Old Testament, pre-Christian prophecy (e.g., *1 Enoch*), or even the "list kept in heaven of those saved and condemned," but probably Jude was making a general reference to the authority of ancient tradition. Taken in this generic sense, their "prewritten condemnation" serves as a topic sentence that categorizes the examples of disobedience (vv. 5-7, 11), the prophecy from *1 Enoch* (vv. 14-15), and the citation of the apostolic predictions (vv.17-18; so Bauckham 1983, 27; Kelly 1981, 249).

The term "were designated" contains an obvious note of predetermination, particularly in the light of the other two instances of "before" language in Jude: Enoch's prior prophecy (v. 14) and the predictions of the apostles (v. 17). In all three, Jude stresses that, on the basis of the knowledge provided by ancient authority, the current opposition has already been identified as deniers of God's truth, hence their fate has been sealed. The saints, those beloved by God, are "kept for Christ" (v. 1) and preserved safe until the second coming (vv. 20, 24). By contrast, the infiltrators are destined only for judgment.

The last part of verse 4 clarifies why "these people" have been condemned. They are "ungodly" people who change the gift of God into "immoral behavior and who deny our Lord and Master Jesus Christ." Jude stresses the destructive nature of ungodliness to make his audience aware of its contours. In this short letter, he uses *asebēs* ("ungodly") three times (here, and twice in v. 15), the cognate noun "ungodliness" *(asebeia)* twice (vv. 15, 18), and the verb form *asebeō* once (v. 15). The terms for ungodliness, though used in Greco-Roman moral discourse, are best understood in light of their Jewish context, especially in the Wisdom literature [LXX], which contrasts the way of life of the *asebeis* ("ungodly") with that of the righteous" (Bauckham 1983, 37). Here, as in the Jewish context, the word group denotes not only individual moral acts but, more, an existential stance which defies God.

Two parallel clauses describe the "ungodliness" of the infiltrators ("those who pervert the grace of our God" and "those who deny our only Master and Lord"). In both clauses Jude suggests that the innovators have turned the saving actions of God, which liberated believers from bondage, into a libertinism, rejecting all constraints. Rather than understanding God's grace as a freedom from sin and for service, the intruders took it as a freedom to indulge their own desire. Similar distortions of God's grace appeared in some of the congregations to which Paul wrote, particularly the church in Corinth (see Rom 6:1, 15: Gal 5:13; and especially 1 Cor 5:1-6; 6:12-30). Bauckham (1983, 38) has suggested the likely possibility that "in both cases [Jude's audience and Corinth] it was Paul's own teaching on Christian freedom from the Law which was exaggerated and distorted."

The word *aselgeia* ("licentiousness") was often used to refer to sexual excess or misconduct. However, *aselgeia* did not always take this sense, so we cannot say that the opponents were actually engaged in sexual misconduct. In fact, in all likelihood they were not. More probably Jude uses the term for its emotional impact and because it implied that the intruders' teaching destroyed the most intimate of behavioral norms. But given the stereotypical use of the term in ancient philosophical polemic, to what inappropriate behavior Jude was referring we cannot really say.

The characterization of the opposition becomes more severe with the second Greek term employed, *arnoumenoi,* which involves denial of, rather than belief in, Jesus as the Lord. For Jude, confession is a matter of commitment and allegiance, not simply verbal expression. Word and deed cannot be divorced, and in separating their utterances of faith from their behavior, the opponents deny Jesus/God as Master and Lord.

The "and" in the phrase "our only Master *and* Lord Jesus Christ" can be either conjunctive or disjunctive. If it is conjunctive (connecting the two phrases), then Master is appositive (defining) to the term "Lord Jesus Christ," so the ungodly are denying Christ as Master. In the second case, taking "and" as disjunctive (contrasting the two phrases as different entities), the ungodly deny both God the Father (i.e., "our only Master") and our Lord Jesus Christ. The author of 2 Peter (who used Jude as a source) understood "and" to connect Christ with God (2 Pet 2:1). However, this is the only certain instance in the New Testament where *despotēs* ("Master") is used of Christ and elsewhere *despotēs* is used of God (Luke 2:29, Acts 4:24, Rev 6:10). Similarly, when *monon* ("only") refers to divine beings, it normally applies to God, as it does in Jude 25. Even though God is called savior there, God clearly is distinguished from Jesus Christ as Lord. Thus in this verse the distinction also was likely intended and Jude was referring to a denial of both God the Master and Christ the Lord (see Bauckham 1983, 39).

In the examples that follow (vv. 5-7), Jude demonstrates how this denial takes place on both volitional and ethical levels. Denial is not outright rejection, but occurs whenever human desire and knowledge are asserted in place of the divine will.

◊ ◊ ◊ ◊

Jude maintained that "contending for the faith" involved not simply mere resistance but also the active integration of beliefs into moral and ethical decisions, i.e., not only a defensive stance, but also proactive behavior. Thus while the response obviously entails a verbal defense against misrepresentation of the gospel, it also demands living in a manner consonant with the gospel's content. The best way to counteract the effects of the intruding opponents was to build a community based on God's truth and strengthened by mutual love, which Jude asserts in the exhortations that end the letter (vv. 20-23).

The intruders also would have used terms common to the faith, but they were not "contending" for it, because, instead of providing a consistent faith, traceable to the beginnings of the Christian message, they advocated innovative ideas that cause deviation from the path of obedience. Innovation *per se* was not Jude's enemy, but fundamental alteration of the truth was, and he perceived the opposition's changes not as extensions of the truth but as its corruption. Because he understood that believers could be deceived, especially from within the community, and that faith could be forfeited, efforts had to be taken to protect the core beliefs and to allow them to flourish. Only diligent adherence to the proclaimed faith could strengthen the church's allegiance and avert the danger of apostasy.

Examples and Arguments (5-19)

Three Examples of Disobedience from the Past (5-7)

This section introduces a series of examples that demonstrates the consequences of opposing God's actions and designs. Jude presents three events, each of which contains three distinctive facets: (1) a relationship with God is established, (2) those given this status refuse to accept it and oppose the will or purpose of God, and (3) this disobedience results in divine judgment. Jude's primary focus in these examples is not the wrath of God; rather, the focus is on the rejection by those who have received God's favor of the responsibilities that their favored status entails. The ancient examples apply directly to the intruders, but they also serve as warnings to the readers that divine favor can be lost through disobedience. Thus, Jude calls on his audience to reflect on their own response to God's mercy.

Jude draws his examples from a traditional schema found in Jewish parenetic material concerning the dire results of apostasy or disobedience (e.g., *Sir* 16:7-10; *CD* 2:16–3:12; 3 Macc 2:4-7). He uses the examples as prophetic types to illustrate and clarify that the intruders, by their disobedience, are placing themselves beyond the pale of the community. While Jude does not state it explicitly, it seems that he wants the congregation to expel the opposition.

A disclosure formula "I desire to remind you," often found in New Testament letters (e.g., Rom 1:13; 1 Cor 10:1; 1 Thess 4:13), introduces the examples (see v. 17, "you must remember"). The phrase "though you are fully informed" modifies the disclosure formula, showing that the judgment of disobedience is inherent in the original narration of the true gospel. Rhetorically, the disclosure formula serves three purposes. First, it embeds Jude's criticisms in ancient wisdom, adding authority to his judgments. Second, it implies that Jude adheres to true belief while the opposition does not. Finally, the disclosure formula warns the congregation to distance themselves from the intruders and their teaching.

◊ ◊ ◊ ◊

Two important interpretive issues arise in verse 5. The first is the placement of *hapax* ("once for all"), and the second is whether the term *kyrios* ("Lord") is a reference to Christ or God. The RSV connects *hapax* with the readers and translates the clause, "Now I desire to remind you, though you were *once for all (hapax)* fully informed." The NRSV, on the other hand, connects the term with God's actions and so reads, "Now I desire to remind you, though you were fully informed that, the Lord, *who once for all (hapax)* saved a people out of the land of Egypt." In the RSV, the "once for all" refers to the knowledge Jude's audience has received and thus is analogous to the "faith that *once for all* was entrusted to the saints" (v. 3). But the NRSV draws an analogy between God's establishment of the eschatological—end time—community through Christ and the people redeemed from captivity in Egypt.

Either translation is possible, but the NRSV fits the context better; *hapax* should be understood here as a quality of God's liberation of Israel. God's action was "once for all" and should have been sufficient for Israel's full deliverance into the promised land, but Israel's disobedience rendered it ineffective. In this way, Israel's past serves as a warning to the current "called ones." God had "once and for all" called Israel out of Egypt, and God has "once for all" acted to deliver the faithful through Christ. In either case, accepting God's salvation means commitment to trust in and serve God. Thus, Jude's statement that those who "did not believe" were destroyed refers to their unwillingness to trust God to sustain them in the wilderness, not to their belief in God as deliverer. Even though they accepted the initial redemptive event, they did not continue to trust God. The implication for his audience is clear: being the beneficiary of God's saving actions means that believers must continue to trust God now and in the future.

Jude's Jewish source material clearly contained the word "Lord" *(kyrios)* as a title for God. But three factors suggest that Jude intended his readers to understand it as a reference to Christ. First, Jude makes the same substitution in verse 14. Second, he has just referred to the "Lord Jesus Christ" in verse 4, and three other times he explicitly connects Jesus Christ with the title "Lord" (vv. 17, 21, 25). Third, the New Testament includes other references to the activity of the pre-existent Christ (e.g., 1 Cor 10:4, 9; Phil 2:6).

Example One: A Disobedient People (5)

Jude's first example draws on Num 14, which recounts the return of Israel's spies from Canaan. When ten of the spies report that the Canaanites' power made the Israelites appear miniscule by comparison, the people complain that their escape from Egypt was futile and that death in captivity would have been a more desirable fate. But Joshua and Caleb identify these complaints as a "rebellion against the Lord" (Num 14:9) and admonish the Israelites to take the land. When the people threaten to stone them, God declares that Israel, the very ones he had rescued, are a people who despise him (Num 14:11). As a result, they will be destroyed and replaced. Jude's expression, "afterward [the Lord] destroyed those who did not believe" (v. 5) alludes to that condemnation (see Num 14:11-12).

The term *to deuteron* ("the second" or "afterward") is difficult to explain since Numbers records no second act of judgment. Probably, we should take it to mean that God's initial act was salvific and that his second act (destruction) follows human rebellion. In the cases of both Israel and the Christian community, God's initial act is deliverance. However, when that act is not properly received, there will be a second moment of divine judgment.

Example Two: The Disobedient Angels (6)

Verse 6 provides a second story of disobedience, which relies on an expansive interpretation of Gen 6:1-4 found in *1 Enoch* 6-19. According to this interpretation, in the primordial period preceding Noah's flood, 200 angels rebelled against God, forsook their place in heaven, and descended to earth (6:14). The angels taught charms and magic spells to earth's inhabitants (7:1-2) and gave them knowledge about weaponry, jewelry, and cosmetics. Subsequently they had intercourse with the women of the earth who bore a hybrid race of "giants." The writer of *1 Enoch* thus declares, "and the world was changed. And there was great impiety and much fornication, and they went astray, and all their ways became corrupt" (*1 Enoch* 8:2). As a result, God flooded the earth to cleanse it of evil and corruption, and the offending angels were imprisoned in darkness (*1 Enoch* 10), until the day of judgment when they will be hurled into fire and destroyed. This entire narrative lies behind Jude's reference in verse 6 (see also 1 Pet 3:19-20; 2 Pet 2:4-5). The angelic rebellion prefigures the disobedience of the infiltrators who represent the same potential for corruption in the community of belief.

The final connection to the story in *1 Enoch* is through the term "kept." The angels Semyaza and Azazel and their accomplices are bound and "kept" in darkness where they remain until the day of judgment (*1 Enoch* 10:4, 12). Jude has repeated the term to link the example of the angels and the first part of verse 6. Since the angels did not "keep" their own place in heaven, they are now "kept" in darkness. Similarly, in Jude, the obedient, who accept their station, are kept for union with Christ (vv. 1, 21), but the disobedient, who rebel against God, are kept for condemnation.

Example Three: Sodom and Gomorrah (7)

In verse 7, Jude provides a third example of disobedience and judgment. He recounts the story of Sodom and Gomorrah which "had long been regarded as the paradigm case of divine judgment (Deut. 29:23; Isaiah 1:9; 13:19; Jer. 23:14; 49:18; 50:40; Lam 4:6; Hosea 11:8; Amos 4:11; Zeph. 2:9; Sir 16:8; 3 Macc 2:5; *Jub.* 16:6, 9; 20:5; 22:22; 36:10; *T. Asher* 7:1; Philo *Quest. In Genesis* 4:51; Josephus *BJ* 5.56. 6; Matt 10:15; 11:24; Mark 11; Luke 10:12; 17:29)" (Bauckham 1983, 53). This example enables Jude to make a second connection between disobedience and sexual misconduct, because like the angels who engaged in illicit intercourse with women (*1 Enoch* 7:1), Sodom's inhabitants also pursued illicit relations. Jude highlights this form of disobedience with his phrase "which, in the same manner as they [the angels], indulged in sexual immorality and pursued unnatural lust" (the allusion occurs already in v. 4).

In the Sodom example, however, the roles of human and divine are reversed. In *1 Enoch*, the angels sought sexual relationships with human beings; but in Gen 19:4 it is the inhabitants of Sodom who attempt to rape the angels. Jude refers to this as "going after other flesh" *(sarkos heteras)*. The author's point here is not that the male inhabitants of Sodom sought to have sex with male visitors, but that they sought relations with angelic beings of an entirely different order. Such intercourse would have transgressed God's ordering of creation and the divine distinction between angels and humans.

Jude's reference to eternal fire also connects the residents of Sodom and the disobedient angels, since eternal fire is the final punishment reserved for both (see *1 Enoch* 10:13-14). Jude's syntax is unclear and either "example" *(deigma)* or "penalty" *(dikē)* could govern the phrase "eternal fire." Since the word *deigma* usually refers to an example which still serves as a proof of divine punishment for later generations, who can still view it (Bauckham 1983, 54), it is particularly apt in this context (see *Wisdom* 10:7). If, on the other hand, "penalty" *(dikē)* governs the phrase, then Jude was arguing that the fires of Sodom and Gomorrah display the severe *degree* of punishment that God would execute. Either option is possible, and each makes an important point. In the first case, Sodom and Gomorrah's punishment is a warning, even in the present. In the second case, the fires remind people that to breach the created order and to violate the boundaries God has established is to provoke divine wrath.

With these three examples Jude illustrates the dire consequences of disobeying God. Disobedience is a form of rebellion, a refusal to accept one's divinely appointed place, and an arrogant reversal of God's ordering. In effect, disobedience is a refusal of God's sovereignty over the universe. The reference to the deliverance of Israel (v. 5) underscores Christ's salvific and judging activities (see also vv. 1, 14, 17, 21, 24-25). The fact that the Lord (Christ) effected the salvation of Israel grounds the present eschatological salvation in God's unified purpose for all people. However, if the Israelites whom Christ had saved disobeyed him and were destroyed, then any member of the present group who denies Christ as Lord can also suffer judgment for disobedience. Through this ancient pattern, one with disastrous consequences, Jude shows that past salvific acts do not preclude future judgment, and a life of faith requires sustaining a trust in and obedience to God (see 1 Cor 10:11 and Heb 3 and 4).

Interpreting the Examples (8)

In verse 8, Jude indicts the intruders for rejecting divine authority, a charge parallel to that of verse 4. The two verses thus frame the thought of the entire section. By repeating "in the same way/manner," "yet," and "also," Jude creates a chain from the primordial disobedience of the angels and the immorality of Sodom to the behavior of the intruders. The pronoun "these" refers to the intruders who are perverting God's grace (v. 4). The words "authority" *(kyrioteta)* and "flesh" recall verse 5 and verse 7, where Jude noted that the people of Israel disobeyed the Lord *(kyrios)* and that the inhabitants of Sodom went after other flesh *(sarkos heteras)*. Defiling the flesh also recalls the angels who "defiled themselves with the women of earth" and hence connects verse 8 to verse 6. Finally, if the expression "slandered the glorious ones" is equivalent to Sodom's treatment of the angels, then verse 8 provides a complete identification of "these intruders" with the disobedient ones of verses 5-7 (so Bauckham 1983, 55).

The use of "yet" makes the connection between verse 8 and verses 5-7 especially clear. The examples of the past were not obscure but known fully to the audience (v. 5) and the intruders. Because they persist in their disobedience despite their knowledge of these examples, the intruders are twice culpable: they are disobedient, and they are also fully cognizant of the consequences.

◊ ◊ ◊ ◊

The participial phrase translated "these dreamers" (which can also mean "these people, in their dreaming") governs all of the verbs in the sentence and suggests that the intruders claimed new insights on the basis of dreams. The "revelations" produce innovations in teaching and behavior, which, the intruders argued, were deeper understandings of the truth, but which Jude took as aberrations of the faith. He therefore levels a three-fold charge against them: (1) they indulge in carnal misbehavior, (2) they vaunt their authority and status, rejecting all other authority, and

(3) they revile the glory of God's agents. In this behavior they repeat the impertinence of Israel, the hubris of the angels, and the immorality of the citizens of Sodom and Gomorrah (vv. 5-7).

The nature of the intruder's dreams is not clear. Most contemporary commentators suggest dreams that reveal divine truths, as in Acts 2:17 (a quotation of Joel 2:28), but the term need not be restricted to "true" revelations. There is a close parallel between this verse and Deut 13:5 which condemns to death a false prophet who is a "dreamer of dreams" and who counsels Israel to "go after other gods" (Deut 13:2).

The charges that the intruders "defile the flesh" and "reject authority" echo the defiant behaviors described in verses 5-7. The verb "defile" occasionally was used for acts of ceremonial pollution, but in conjunction with "the flesh" it takes on the meaning of sexual immorality, as it does in Philo and Josephus (BDAG, 650). Jude likely has this connotation in mind, but his opponents would not have considered their actions lustful indulgences, but expressions of their God-given freedom. Hence, they did not "reject authority" but upheld it with their behavior.

The final charge, "they revile the glorious ones" *(doxas)* presents a minor interpretive puzzle because the identity of the "glorious ones" is not clear. Commentators have offered numerous alternatives (leaders of the community, good angels, and evil spirits); the expression most likely refers to angelic beings (Kelly 1981, 263). The following verse, which suggests a similar form of insubordination, supports this likelihood (see comment on 2 Pet 2:10). In Jewish thought, "glory" *(doxa)* properly belonged to God alone. Eventually, however, the "glory of God" came to be associated with the angelic cohort that surrounded God, and they were considered to share in this glory (Kelly 1981, 263, who cites Heb 9:5, *T. Levi* 13:5, *T. Jud* 25:2).

◊ ◊ ◊ ◊

If the identity of the "glorious ones" is somewhat obscure, Jude's point is not. The intruders do not understand the magnitude or source of the power that they oppose. Like early Israel (v.

5), they presume to understand more than they do and so erroneously assert their superiority over the angels of God. The same dynamic is apparent in the phrase *kyriotēta de athetousin* ("reject authority"). The term *kyriotēta* recalls the rejection of the Lord *(kyrios)* mentioned in verse 5, and the initial charge of verse 4 is that the intruders deny our Lord *(kyrios)* Jesus Christ. The term "reject" signifies a refusal to recognize authority and efforts to set it aside. This pride was clearly the sin of the angels in verse 6 and implicitly that of Israel and the citizens of Sodom (see 1 Thess 4:3-8). For Jude, no worse offense can occur than the denial of God's created order and edicts, especially under the pretense of spiritual insight.

A Type-Antitype Example (9-10)

While verses 5-8 assert that the opposition repeats the ancient behavior of disobedience, verses 9-10 contrast them to an example of obedience and deference. The author refers to the legend of the dispute over the corpse of Moses. According to the legend, the Devil charges that Moses, having slain an Egyptian (Exod 2:12), was a murderer. As a consequence, he opposed Moses' burial and claimed that the corpse belonged to him. The archangel Michael and the Devil then enter into a legal dispute over Moses' body.

Speculation concerning Moses' burial stemmed from a cryptic remark in Exodus 34:6, "He was buried in a valley in the land of Moab, opposite Bethpeor, but no one knows his burial place to this day." The story recounted in Jude is not found in the Old Testament, nor is Jude's source extant. Clement of Alexandria identified it as the *Assumption of Moses*, but most modern commentators consider the *Testament of Moses* more likely (see Bauckham 1983, 65-76 for a full discussion). Unfortunately, the extant versions of both these texts are fragmentary, and no conclusions can be drawn about their precise content (Neyrey 1993, 66).

◊ ◊ ◊ ◊

Michael's pronouncement, "The Lord rebuke you!" (v. 9), originally comes from Zech 3:2, but it was likely contained in Jude's Jewish source. In Zechariah, Satan is rebuffed in his accusations of Joshua the High Priest, and Jude has adopted the rebuke here. Some interpreters view the rebuke as a "mild imprecation," but this does not do justice to the level of condemnation. The term "rebuke" often was used to refer to censure of opponents by someone with superior power and authority (e.g., Mark 1:25 and 4:39). Lexical evidence suggests "punish" as a possible translation of the verb in this verse (BDAG, 384).

In Zech 3:2 and in Jude's Jewish source, kyrios ("the Lord") would have referred to God. As in verse 5, however, Jude probably intended "Lord" to mean Jesus Christ, and transformed Michael's request into a call on the "Lord (Jesus)" to rebuke Satan. Thus, in contrast to the opposition, Michael does not exceed his station, but defers to the Master. Michael does not forget that he is only an advocate. So he refrains from judging the Devil and "does not presume to bring a condemnation of slander against him" (Bauckham 1983, 60; Kelly 1981, 264).

The phrasing and structure of verse 10 demonstrates the dual failings of the opposition. Despite their claims to divine wisdom, the intruders are stupid and brutish. Though they prefer to understand themselves as competitors of the angels, they are mere human beings, devoid of insight, and driven by carnal impulse (BDAG, 1069). They are like animals capable of responding to physical urges but incapable of transcending them by thought or spiritual discipline. As a result, they confuse the indulgence of physical impulses with true freedom derived from a right relationship with God. In the end they are condemned by their vile natures and by their deep resistance to truth (see v. 5).

◊ ◊ ◊ ◊

Michael, whose name means "who is like God," is a chief angel, entrusted with the role of protecting God's people (Dan 12:1). One tradition that illumines Jude's reference to him is found in *1 Enoch* 40, where Enoch relates seeing "an innumerable and uncountable (multitude) who stand before the glory of the Lord of the Spirits" (*1 Enoch* 40:1). In this countless throng, four angelic faces appear, Michael first among them (*1 Enoch* 40:9). Of all divine servants, Michael holds the greatest authority and stands closest to God. He is God's emissary who challenges other angelic beings (*1 Enoch* 10:11), and so he is designated as the Devil's adversary (cf. Rev 12:17). Michael is thus a perfect counter-example to the instances of transgression recorded in verses 5-7.

The intruders, who clearly do not have Michael's privilege of rank, still reviled "beings of glory" and so transgress their God-ordained position. Unlike Michael, they do not understand that only God has the status to rebuke angels. In arrogance they ignore the power differential that exists between divine beings and mortal ones.

Jude thus repeats the warnings of the previous examples. All beings, human and divine, must maintain respectful deference toward God. It is not a claim of privileged status, but a proper understanding of the role and station God has assigned that demonstrates faithfulness.

Examples from Scripture (11)

Verses 11-13 continue the criticism begun in verses 5-10 and amplify the characterizations of the intruders found in verses 8 and 10. While the descriptions are still too general to produce a fine-grained portrait of the opposition, they are more specific than the previous criticisms and suggest a group that considered itself more spiritually elevated than their fellow believers.

◊ ◊ ◊ ◊

In verse 11, Jude adopts a prophetic "woe oracle" to compare the opposition to new examples of sin and error. This form originated with Israel's prophets who typically used it as an announcement of doom. In its fullest form the oracle had three parts: (1) a proclamation of woe, (2) the specific behaviors that prompt the pronouncement, and (3) a statement of judgment.

While Jude follows this basic structure, he amplifies it by the multiplication of exemplars. The proclamation of woe is uttered in 11*a* and then is followed by a series of three charges and judgments (11*b*, *c*).

By employing the oracle form, Jude signals that the intruders' errors are ultimate violations of God's designs, which will result in judgment and destruction. Once more, Jude illustrates the intruders' behavior and judgment with examples from Israel's past (Cain, Balaam, and Korah). With each example, the defiant behavior incurs a more severe penalty.

One tradition of post-biblical Judaism depicted Cain's self-love, greed, and defiance of God, portraying him as the epitome of jealousy, envy, and self-indulgence (e.g., Philo, *Mig. Abr.* 75 and Josephus, *Ant.* 1:52-53). Though these are generic charges, they make Jude's point. Like Cain, the infiltrators are falsely self-reliant, they misunderstand the nature of real faith, and "give themselves over to godlessness and sensuality and are doomed to eternal corruption" (Kelly 1981, 266-267).

Jude depicts the second figure, Balaam, as driven by an unquenchable desire for wealth. Jude does not rely on Num 22-24, but on a later Jewish exposition of Num 31:15-16 that portrays Balaam as a greedy deceptive teacher, whose advice led Israel into immorality and idolatry (Josephus, *Ant.* 4.129). As a result, he was slain by an army raised to avenge Israel. Jude has modified the emphasis of the tradition, focusing on Balaam's avarice rather than on his bad advice, in order to highlight that the intruders were demanding payment for their teaching. His reference to "gain" suggests that they were not motivated by truth but by money, implying that they were insincere and that their teaching was tainted. The intruders "abandon themselves" (BDAG, 312) to Balaam's error. They cannot resist the temptation of financial profit. Hence, they stray from the truth and ignore the welfare of their audience for the sake of personal gain.

The last comparison, to Korah, is the most devastating in Jude's series. According to Numbers 16, Korah, along with Dathan and Abiram, led 250 people in a rebellion against Moses and Aaron. Because of their verbal opposition to God's ordained laws, God punished them with swift and definitive judgment. The earth opened and swallowed Korah, Dathan, and Abiram, along with their households (Num 16:30-33). At almost the same moment, fire dropped from the heavens, and flames consumed the 250 who joined in the confrontation.

Jude states that the opposition "perishes in Korah's rebellion." The verb choice matches their audacity with that of the original rebellion, and the present tense of the verb underscores that the judgment has already been made. The intruders do not simply die; they are utterly eliminated. Although God's punishment may not appear as quickly as it did in Korah's case, it is just as certain and just as severe.

◊   ◊   ◊   ◊

The woe oracle in verse 11 thus serves two purposes in Jude's argument. First, in choosing this form, Jude identifies himself with the ancient prophets and lends authority to his statements. Second, the use of the oracle suggests that Jude, like the prophets, must awaken an audience to a peril it does not recognize. Like his prophetic precursors, Jude uses metaphor and poetry, as well as shocking examples, to alert them to the danger. Jude indicates that his readers must heed his description of the opposition if they wish to survive spiritually. For despite their benign outward appearance, the intruders are as ruthless as Cain, as corrupt as Balaam, and as rebellious as Korah.

By means of these comparisons, Jude places the intruders in the company of arch-villains and connects their condemnation with the fate of their predecessors. The disobedient behaviors become increasingly worse. The opposition *follows* the way of Cain, they *abandon* themselves to Balaam's error, and finally they *perish* with Korah. Commensurately, the forms of punishments also escalate: Cain is cursed; Balaam is slain by another human being; and Korah perishes directly and immediately, solely through God's action. By ending with Korah's rebellion, Jude emphasizes the serious nature of denying God as sovereign. Jude began the letter with this charge (v. 4) and underscored it with the examples recorded in verses 6-10. With verse 11 he places it directly in front of the audience. The intruders are revealed as corrupters of the community by their rebellion; they are opponents of God, whose destruction is as sure and severe as that of Korah.

THE TRUE NATURE OF THE OPPOSITION REVEALED (12-13)

In verses 12-13 Jude uses metaphors drawn from nature to reveal that the speech and deeds of the intruders are hollow, mere appearances of truth with no substance. Their conduct will distort God's church just as evil warps the natural design of God's creation.

◊   ◊   ◊   ◊

Blemishes on their Love-Feasts (12a)

Jude's first image portrays the opposition as "blemishes on your love-feasts." The NRSV translates the Greek term *spilades* as "blemishes," but notes that the term "reefs" is also possible. Commentators are divided between the two. Those who translate *spilades* as "blemish" or "stain" point to verse 23, where a similar verb refers to "tunics spotted (or defiled) by the flesh." They also note that in the parallel passage (2 Pet 2:13), the related term *spiloi* ("blemishes") refers to the intruders, which suggests that the author of the later letter understood Jude to mean "blemish" or "stain."

Despite this evidence, there are reasons to prefer the translation "reefs" or "rocks." First, the term regularly designates a rock on the shoreline or in the sea (BDAG, 938). In contrast, there is only one known instance where the term takes the meaning "spot" or "blemish" (Orpheus, *Lithica* 614; Mayor 1965, 41; BDAG, 938). Second, when the term is allowed this usual sense, a comparison between the opposition and rocks or shoals becomes evident. Thus, just as rocks can destroy a ship, taking its passengers to certain ruin, so the opposition's mere presence in the "agape feast" is sufficient to wreak havoc in the community. Only if the readers exercise caution and keep the opposition in view can they avoid destruction (see Bauckham 1983, 85-86).

The term *agapais*, "love-feasts," refers to communal meals eaten by believers in celebration of their common bonds and commitments. The meal, a celebration of God's love for the community and its members' mutual love for one another, often included the Eucharist and was a significant moment of reverence and intimacy. The opposition's presence at such meals indicates how deeply they have infiltrated the community's life.

Jude's critique of the intruders centers on the attitude they adopted toward God and the community. He points out that "these people feast among you without fear," since they show no reverence for God. As a result, they cannot really participate in a meal dedicated to thanking God. Bauckham (1983, 86) suggests that the term "without fear" "probably relates to the spiritual arrogance of the false teachers, who behave as though they were their own masters, not subject to the Lord." The opposition also showed a disdain for the congregation. By separating themselves they deny the unity Christ created in the church by his death, and once again "deny our only Master and Lord" (v. 4; see 1 Cor 11:18-20).

The intruders' self-indulgent actions also display their lack of respect toward God (and Christ) and the congregation. Though the NRSV translates *syneuōchoumenoi* as "feeding themselves," it also recognizes an alternative: "shepherds who care only for themselves." It is likely that Jude had this second idea in mind, since the idea of feeding oneself could be expressed more conventionally, and the term "shepherd" was often used in early Christian groups to refer to church leaders (John 21:16; 1 Pet 5:2; Eph 4:11). Notwithstanding the intruders' wish to be spiritual guides and leaders, they disqualified themselves through their selfish and self-serving behavior.

The description of the intruders as self-indulgent shepherds is probably an allusion to Ezek 34:2. There, Ezekiel reports a command from the Lord to speak against Israel's leaders who have allowed the people to be decimated while they themselves grow fat and wealthy. God condemns these "shepherds" for their self-indulgence and removes them from their posts. In a similar manner, the intruders prosper but only at the expense of those they claim to be serving.

Images from Nature (12*b*-13)

The images found in verses 12*b*-13 (clouds, winds, trees, waves, and stars) are drawn from the portion of *1 Enoch* that follows Jude's quotation from *1 Enoch* 1:9 (vv. 14-15; so Mayor 1965, 42). *First Enoch* contrasts the "obedient" stars, clouds, trees, and seas to those who transgress the God-given law. Since God created human beings and the cosmic elements of the universe, when either violate the divine course set for them, their true form or function becomes warped and distorted.

Once again Jude adapts the traditional material to his argument, appropriating imagery from *1 Enoch,* but applying the metaphors differently. Unlike *1 Enoch,* where the natural elements stand in contrast to human rebellion, in Jude the intruders are depicted as natural entities that have gone awry: blossoming trees that bear no fruit and storm clouds that produce no rain. Because of their disobedience to the designs of God, whatever they say or do results only in empty promises. The metaphors equate the lack of spiritual sustenance with the unnatural famine and drought. As corrupted sources, the intruders cannot produce nourishment, and the community's vitality will wither.

◊ ◊ ◊ ◊

Waterless Clouds (12b)

Jude first portrays the opponents as "waterless clouds carried by winds." Though the clouds promise relief and bounty, their appearance is a deception. Similarly, the intruders appear to offer benefit for the congregation, but their promises are never filled, and the hopes they encourage are always disappointed. In addition, the cloud imagery displays the ephemeral and transient nature of the teachers. There is no permanence to the clouds; they go where the wind directs and evaporate as soon as they appear. Likewise, the intruders have no permanence, and with the next impulse (or most likely the next opportunity) they will leave the community for another set of naïve listeners (see e.g., Eph 4:14).

Fruitless Trees (12c)

The second image compares the opposition to "autumn trees, without fruit, twice dead, uprooted." Jude highlights the notion of unfulfilled promise once more but adds a condemnatory note: the intruders will be sentenced and destroyed. The term "autumn" is a difficult one to make precise. Some commentators think it refers to a time after the regular harvest when trees are not expected to bear fruit. Jude added the phrase to "spell out the full significance of their [the intruders] condition: they are trees from which, sapless and sterile as they are, no fruit can be looked for" (Kelly 1981, 272). Mayor, however, argues that the term applies to a late autumn harvest in which the last ripe fruit is gleaned from trees (Mayor 1965, 55-59). In this case, the opponents fail to provide something they should have produced. This interpretation fits well with the context, creating a parallel between the trees and the clouds. Just as waterless clouds promise rain but do not deliver, so these trees, which should provide nourishment, yield nothing.

Jude extends the harvest metaphor by calling the trees "twice dead" and "uprooted." The sense of "twice dead" comes not from agriculture, but from Jude's characterization of the opposition as internally dead and externally non-productive; hence, twice dead. One should never look to these "trees" for produce because, despite their outward appearance, they are already dead at their core. The opposition's lack of genuine teaching and sincere acts of faith is not a temporary lapse, but a signal of a permanent state.

The phrase "twice dead" may also allude to the Last Judgment when the deeds of humanity will be judged and the ultimate fate of each person is revealed (Rev 2:11; 20:6, 14; 21:8). As disobedient rebels, the intruders are spiritually dead, and their ultimate judgment is preordained. They are thus dead with respect to the present and to the future.

Since they are dead and useless trees, they are uprooted. This motif, found elsewhere in the New Testament (Matt 3:10; 7:19; John 15:2-6), often refers to judgments rendered for failing to produce what is reasonably expected. Trees, rightly tended, should produce fruit, and believers, who rightly understand God, should manifest their faith in their speech and actions. The intruders fail this test, and like trees which do not produce fruit, they will be uprooted and destroyed.

Wild Waves and Wandering Stars (13)

Verse 13 contains two final metaphors that highlight what Kelly (1981, 274) calls the "moral degeneracy" of the false teachers. Perhaps the phrase "moral degeneracy" is too strong, but Jude does impress upon the congregation the thorough nature of their impurity. By employing the imagery of the crashing waves (13a) and wandering stars (13b), he indicates that when the opponents finally act, they are more likely to harm or defile the community than to help it.

The expression, "wild waves of the sea" recalls imagery used in Isa 57:20 (see also *Wisdom* 14:1). There the image contrasts the peace of the righteous with the unrest of the wicked. The wicked are anxious and constantly in motion, like a tossing sea that disturbs the ocean floor. Jude focuses on this activity and depicts the intruders as savagely and chaotically out of control. The rare verb "casting up the foam," which refers to the splashing motion of sea foam tossed in the air (BDAG, 360), suggests that the shameless deeds of the opposition are flung about aimlessly, like a stormy ocean that casts debris on a shore. Jude thus depicts their teaching as unfocused and disordered, the result of a frenzy that knows no bounds or purpose.

Jude ends this set of metaphors by comparing the intruders to "wandering stars," a term borrowed from *1 Enoch* (*1 Enoch* 80:6). The figure reflects the apocalyptic notion that angels control the stars and planets (Bauckham 1983, 89). According to this strand of ancient thought, the stars normally followed regular orbits and patterns and, when they did not, the variations were attributed to disobedience among the heavenly ranks (*1 Enoch* 18:14-16). Ultimately, the disobedient spirits who caused the stars' distorted paths are judged for their transgressions and imprisoned in a deep and endless chasm, "bound until the time of the consummation of their sin" (*1 Enoch* 18:16). In addition, according to common Greek thought, the planets were stars that "wandered," "planet" deriving from the verb *planeō* ("to wander"). By using this language, Jude reveals that the intruders wander from God's ordained paths. The comparison to the erratic stars allows Jude to create a word play between "wandering" (*planētai*) and "error" *planē*, used when charging the intruders with Balaam's error (v. 11). Like stars gone amuck, the intruders blunder in error, misleading those they teach and influence. For this they are judged and condemned to "a deepest darkness," kept specifically for their punishment. Here Jude adapts imagery found in *1 Enoch* 21, where the stars that transgressed the commands of the Lord are imprisoned because of their sin and consigned to a fiery abyss. Jude speaks of a "dark abyss," referring back to the image of verse 6. He thereby connects the fate of the intruders with that of the angels who transgressed God's order by abandoning their designated heavenly place.

With these metaphors, and indeed, throughout the whole letter, Jude has emphasized that when God's designs and purposes for the world are transgressed, the natural order is subverted, producing only hollow forms that cannot sustain life. In their arrogance, the intruders deny the sovereignty of God and disobey the divine ordinances. Like abnormalities in nature, they are aberrations in the community. Moreover, their self-indulgence and disregard for the wellbeing of the others harms the congregation. The speech of the opponents is pernicious and shameful, not only because it is false, but also because it disappoints and misleads. Worse than merely being arid or sterile, they pollute the community and threaten its very existence.

A PROPHECY FROM ENOCH (14-16)

Verses 14-16 provide the first of two criticisms based on citations from ancient authorities. Both criticisms follow a similar pattern: Jude first cites the authority (vv. 14-15, 17-18) and then identifies the opposition as those the citation condemns (v. 16, 19). Jude's use of "these are" (vv. 14, 16, 19) and the terms "prophesied" *(proephēteusen, v. 14)* and "predictions" *(proeirēmenon, v. 17)*, both of which refer to announcements made prior to the actual events they report, connect the two criticisms.

The Prophecy Quoted (14-15)

With the quotation in verses 14-15 drawn from *1 Enoch* 1:9, Jude establishes that his assessments of the intruders are grounded in the words of the prophet Enoch. In the New Testament there are few specific references to Enoch (Luke 3:37; Heb 11:5), and no New Testament writer is as indebted to *1 Enoch* as Jude is. Nevertheless, Enoch traditions had a significant influence on the theological and exegetical developments of the early Church. The enigmatic statement that, "Enoch walked with God; and then he was no more, because God took him" (Gen 5:24), implies that Enoch did not die but was taken from the earth while still alive. Later Jewish interpreters focused on Enoch's privileged status and developed the idea that he was privy to God's will and wisdom. They argued that by divine sanction, Enoch could reveal this knowledge to human beings still on earth. Elements of the tradition extended from Jewish apocalyptic thought into early Christian writings, including Jude.

Drawing on the genealogy recorded in Gen 5:1-24, Jude refers to Enoch as "the seventh from Adam." He has employed a Semitic form of counting that begins with the progenitor, hence: Adam, Seth, Enosh, Kenan, Mahalalel, Jared, Enoch (see *1 Enoch* 60:8 and 93:3). The point is not to express Enoch's age or to venerate him as an ancient, but to stress the number seven, considered in Hebrew and Christian thinking to be a perfect and climactic number. As the "seventh" one, Enoch is uniquely blessed, and his words are worthy of special attention.

First Enoch 1:2 reads, "this is a holy vision from the heavens. . . . I look not for this generation but for the distant one that is coming. I speak about the elect ones and concerning them." Jude takes this statement literally and understands that Enoch's prophecy is about Jude's own time, specifically about those who are corrupting the believing community. As a result, he changes *1 Enoch's* statement about God's theophany, God's presence seen in a vision, into a prophecy about Christ's second coming, substituting the noun *kyrios* ("Lord") for *1 Enoch's* term "the one" (which referred to God). Jude is again exploiting the ambiguity of the term "Lord," this time in order to connect Enoch's prophecy with the belief that Jesus would return at the end of the age to render judgment on humanity (Matt 25:31-46; Mark 13:24-27).

An early Christian tradition that Christ would return with a holy army to vanquish the unholy (Mark 8:39, Matt 16:27, Luke 9:26) influences Jude here. This concept harks back to symbols of power and authority associated with God's retinue in the Hebrew Bible (e.g., Ps 68:17, Deut 33:2, Zech 14:5). Early Christian belief transfers this power to the Christ, who returns as conquering Lord, establishing his reign over all other authorities.

The context of *1 Enoch* 1:9 suggests that God's judgment will be passed on "all flesh" i.e., all the inhabitants of earth, righteous and ungodly (*1 Enoch* 1:7). But "all" for Jude refers only to all those who commit ungodly deeds. He thereby underscores the adverse judgment that will be passed on the "ungodly," particularly the intruders.

The quotation's conclusion focuses on the "ungodliness" of those who are judged, as the triple repetition of the word group shows: all people are judged for their "deeds of *ungodliness*," done in an "*ungodly* way," and for the harsh speech against God that they spoke as "*ungodly* sinners." Jude employs the term *sklēros* ("hard") not to suggest that the intruders' speech was difficult to understand, but to indicate that it was harsh or impudent, i.e., speech used with demeaning intent (vv. 8, 10). The harsh things spoken against God connects the prophecy with the resistant speech of the opponents.

The Prophecy Applied to the Intruders (16)

Following *1 Enoch*'s lead, Jude divides the intruders' disobedience into speech and deeds. In the first part of the letter, Jude has focused on the misdeeds of the intruders, though he has alluded to their barren speech in verses 12-13. In verse 16 he refers directly to their ungodly speech, already insinuated in verse 15. Jude's use of "grumblers" and "malcontents," both found only here in the New Testament, strengthens the critique. The noun "grumblers" is used in Num 14:2, 27, 29, 36 to describe the Israelites who complained about life in the wilderness after escaping from Egypt. The speech of the intruders is also a form of "grumbling" against God, evidence of the same sins of disobedience and lack of trust in God.

The next two phrases describe the corollaries of refusing to trust in God. Rather than trusting in God, the intruders "live according to their own desires" *(kata tas epithymias heautōn poreuomenoi)*. The NRSV's translation "they indulge in their own lusts" suggests an emphasis on sexual appetites and sexual misconduct, but Jude's indictment included more than this. The word desires *(epithymias)* need not, and often does not, have a sexual meaning except in particular contexts. Given his consistent contrast of ungodliness to a mindset that affirms God's design, "following their own desires" appears to be Jude's way of describing the intruders' complete rebellion against God (so Bauckham 1983, 98; compare with Kelly 1981, 278). This interpretation is consistent with the sense of the same phrase in verse 18 (see comment).

The second phrase, which translated literally is "their mouth speaks haughty words" (NRSV: "they are bombastic in speech"), reveals how the opponents' manner of teaching expresses their disposition. The repetition of the verb "speak" (v. 15) makes this phrase another interpretation of "the harsh things ungodly sinners have spoken against him," enabling Jude to show the vacuity and arrogance of the intruders. The intruders not only display misplaced confidence in their own abilities and thought, but they do so in direct defiance of God. Again we are reminded of the indictments of the intruders as "those who revile what they do not understand" (vv. 9-10).

The last phrase, *thaumazontes prōsopa ōpheleias charin* (NRSV: "flattering people to their own advantage") occurs only here in the New Testament. Because it is a parenthetical remark, Jude's use of the phrase and its semantic connection to the two clauses that precede it are not entirely clear.

The phrase *prosōpa ōpheleias charin* is actually a Greek translation of an idiom occurring often in the Hebrew Bible, *nasa' panim*, "to raise the countenance" (e.g., Gen 19:21; Lev 19:15; Deut 10:17, 28; 2 Chron 19:7; Job 13:10; 22:8; Prov. 18:5). Initially it referred to an ancient custom of greeting. When two people met, one would prostrate himself (the custom referred most often to men), and the other would raise the first one's face so that they might look at each other, expressing a mutual acceptance (Lohse 1968, 779-780). The expression signified the preference given to those with social status and wealth, but could also refer to the partiality shown to those who offered bribes and favors. Thus, the term could have a defamatory tone, which Jude intends here. In contrast to this social construction of human value, biblical writers often refer to God as one who shows no partiality (see Deut 10:17, 2 Chron 19:7; Acts 10:34; Rom 2:11).

The characterization of the intruders as "flattering people to their own advantage" means that the intruders showed preference to certain members of the congregation in order to gain their acceptance. Those that advanced their standing with the congregation were courted; those who could not or would not were ignored. Thus, the intruders are charged one last time with an arrogant self-indulgence that ignores the honor of God and compromises the truth for the sake of human acceptance (see Jas 2:1-9 and 2 Cor 2:17).

◊   ◊   ◊   ◊

The quotation from *1 Enoch* commended itself to Jude because it foretells God's judgment on the "ungodly" who "deny the name of the Lord of the Spirits" and rebel against the Lord's designs (*1 Enoch* 38:2, 41:2, 45:2, 46:6, 48:10; see also Charles 1993, 161). The quotation in verses 14-15 recalls the indictment of verse 4, as the words "ungodly" and "judgment" show. *1 Enoch* identifies both the actions *and* the speech of the rebellious ones as causes for their condemnation. "Ungodliness" is not merely a collection of actions or utterances, but a state of disobedience. Thus, the error of the intruders is not remediable (vv. 12-13), and their behavior and speech mark their true essence (v. 16).

THE APOSTOLIC PREDICTIONS (17-19)

Up to this point, the chief object of Jude's attention has been the character and actions of the intruders. However, in verses 17-19 Jude's tone changes and his focus shifts. The intruders remain a concern (v. 18), but it is the needs of the readers that receive his direct attention from here through the end of the letter. The exhortations that begin with this verse are intended to help the audience strengthen itself as a community.

◊ ◊ ◊ ◊

The phrase "but you, beloved" (v. 17) recalls the salutation in verse 3 and signals the shift in focus. The affectionate term stands in sharp contrast to the expressions "they" or "these" used to identify the opposition and reminds the audience that they are of a different character than the intruders.

The imperative of the verb "must remember" also announces a transition. Jude began his illustrations of the consequences of disobedience with the same verb (v. 5). Using the examples of Israel and Sodom and Gomorrah, he reminded the audience that the intruders were the most recent version of an ancient case of disbelief. Now, in verse 17, he instructs the audience to recall another set of teachings that make the same identification: the apostolic predictions. He thus creates a continuous thread between the traditions from God's earliest encounter with Israel (vv. 5-7), through the authority of the prophets (vv.

14-15), to the recent agents of the proclamation of Jesus as Lord.

The apostolic warning that Jude cites not only shows the continuity of his charges with ancient and recent authorities, it also contains a two-fold form of exhortation. First, the presence of the intruders should not surprise the readers, because the apostles had already foretold the appearance of scoffers and apostates. Second, the very appearance of the intruders is itself a sign of the truthfulness of the apostolic preaching. Indeed, the fulfilled prediction shows God's complete sovereignty, because even God's opponents accomplish God's designs. Thus, by this ironic twist the scoffers who were a danger, finally become, despite themselves, aids to the congregation's faith.

Given the manner in which Jude used Enoch's prophecy and the examples drawn from other forms of authority (vv. 5, 7, 11, 14), it is not necessary to take the terms "the apostles" or "they said to you" as a historical reference to actual instruction. Rather, just as Enoch "spoke" of the present situation, so the apostles "spoke" of it in their initial preaching. The phrase is simply Jude's way of investing the apostles with the same "prophetic" authority given to the other ancient witnesses. All of God's authorities, ancient and recent, written or spoken, have foretold the presence of corrupting intruders. When the congregation remembers this, it will realize that it has been forewarned and that God has provided the resources to resist those who try to corrupt the truth (vv. 3, 5).

The general content of the warning provides additional evidence for this interpretation. The apostles are said only to have taught that, "in the last time there will be scoffers, indulging their own ungodly lusts"; no specific source, however, is cited. Nothing in early Christian literature matches this quotation verbatim, except 2 Pet 3:13, whose author copied it from Jude. The wording of verse 18 recalls the language of verse 16, particularly the phrase "indulging their own lusts." The term "ungodly" (v. 18) recalls "the actions of the ungodly" (vv. 4, 15).

Predictions about some future appearance of false teachers or scoffers occur often in the New Testament (Mark 13:21-23;

Matt 24:24-25; Acts 10:29-30; 1 Tim 4:1-3; 2 Tim 3:1-9; 1 John 2:18-19; also *Did.* 16:3-4). The prevalence of this tradition indicates that it had become part of early Christian teaching and that attribution to the apostles cannot be taken as a reference to a specific text. Jude adopts the tradition here, modifying it, particularly with the terms "desires" and "ungodly," and attributes it to the apostles in general.

Three expressions in verse 18 require specific attention: the words "scoffers" and "the last time" and the phrase "indulging their own ungodly lusts." In the New Testament, the term "scoffers" occurs only here and at 2 Pet 3:3 (for cognate terms, see Heb 11:36 and Matt 27:29, 31; 27:41 and parallels). In the Old Testament Wisdom material, the "scoffer" is one who shows disdain for wisdom and morality (Prov 1:1, 14:6; Ps 35:16). Jude uses the term to emphasize that the opponents are not simply wrong but that they arrogantly assert themselves over against received wisdom and truth (vv. 10, 16).

In the prophetic tradition of the Old Testament, the phrase "in the last time" refers to the moment when God finally would mete out judgment and salvation (e.g., Isa 2:2-4; Hos 3:5). In apocalyptic thought, the "last time" came to represent the time immediately prior to the commencement of God's public reign when God would establish divine justice, reward the righteous, and punish the wicked. New Testament writers appropriated this eschatological sense and applied it to the time inaugurated by the life, death, and resurrection of Jesus (Heb 1:2; Acts 2:17; Gal 1:4), but prior to his second coming (1 Cor 1:8; 15:51-54; 2 Thess 1:7-8; 2 Pet 3:4). Since the appearance of false prophets and "scoffers" was a sign that Christ's return was imminent (e.g., Mark 13:22), Jude likely was using the phrase to present the appearance of the intruders as evidence that he and his readers were living at the close of the age. Hence, they should live faithfully, awaiting the second coming of Christ with expectant hope (vv. 1, 21).

As in verse 16, the NRSV again translates *kata tas heautōn epithymias poreuomenoi* as "indulging their own ungodly lusts." The syntax actually suggests "following their own desires for ungodliness," and, once more, interpretative caution is required. The phrase is even more complex than verse 16 because Jude has added the plural form of the noun "ungodliness." The Greek syntax can be taken in one of two ways: either (1) "ungodliness" modifies "desires"—thus, "ungodly desires" with the emphasis falling on desires that are themselves ungodly, or (2) "desires" which have "ungodliness" as their goal. The second alternative is preferable. Taken this way, ungodliness is not restricted to immorality. Rather, immoral desires are only one form of the rebellious behavior that stems from desires to resist God (Bauckham 1983, 105).

Jude's typical and demeaning pronoun "these" connects verses 18 and 19 so that verse 19 illustrates the "desires for ungodliness" of verse 18. Jude calls the opposition "worldly" and "devoid of the Spirit" and charges them with producing schisms in the congregation. The divisive behavior reveals their true nature; they are physically-based individuals who do not possess the gift of the Spirit.

In the first clause, Jude asserts that the scoffers "create division" in the community. Jude uses this extremely rare verb (found only here in the New Testament) to condemn the intruders' actions in the church. No matter what they claim, their presence splinters the congregation and harms the community. Jude does not address the exact form of the divisions and the basis on which they were made, but rather the severe conditions they created. Perhaps he has in mind the factions (implied in v. 12) by which the intruders ruined the "agape" meals. The divisions provide more evidence that the intruders neither understand God's economy of unity nor work to maintain it.

Jude also denounces the opposition as "worldly people." The term is used in contrast to people who possess the Spirit (v. 20), as the additional phrase "those not having the Spirit" shows. By "worldly," Jude implies that the opposition does not belong to the ranks of the faithful. Just as the ungodly do not obey the precepts of God, so the "worldly ones" are motivated by this world's array of values (see Jas 3:15). The intruders, at their core, are driven by desires for prestige, gain, and selfishness.

The intruders are "devoid of the Spirit" (v. 19). The gift of God's Spirit established someone as a member of God's elect community (2 Cor 1:22; Eph 1:13-14; Gal 4:6; 5:25). The Spirit brought wellbeing and discernment, provided insight to understand God's truth (1 Cor 2:9-13), and enabled God's people to communicate their innermost thoughts in prayer (Rom 8:26-27). The Spirit also provided the gifts and graces that maintained unity (1 Cor 12:4-11). Because they were "devoid of the Spirit" the opposition could not comprehend God's truth, nor participate in the congregation's ministries or communion.

EXHORTATION TO ACTS OF FAITHFULNESS (20-23)

In verse 3 Jude declared his initial intention to write about the commonly shared salvation. However, the need to counteract the influence of intruders on the spiritual health of the community forced him to the polemics of verses 4-19 instead. Nevertheless, polemic was not Jude's ultimate purpose for writing. Ultimately, Jude desired that the congregation pursue a life of obedience and fidelity to God. The exposure of the intruders' false teaching and the demonstration of its ethical implications provided one form of contending for the faith. In verses 20-23, Jude returns to his initial exhortation and states a second dimension of contending for the faith: acting in accord with faith. In many ways, verses 20-23 form the core of Jude's letter—an appeal for the entire church to exercise communal aspects of a life of faith.

General Exhortations (20-21)

In verse 3 Jude addressed his audience as "beloved" and admonished them "to contend for the faith that was entrusted to the saints." In verse 20 he again addresses the readers as "beloved" and implores them to build upon the foundation of their "holy faith" *(hagiōtatē pistei)*. The word play on *hagioi* ("saints," v. 3), and *hagiōtatē* ("most holy," v. 20) links verses 20-23 to the initial goals of Jude's letter. In contrast to the worldly intruders who live without the Spirit (v. 19), Jude indicates that the Spirit empowers the "beloved" (v. 20). The opposition creates divisions; "the beloved," on the other hand, build one another up on the holy faith.

Jude exhorts his readers to follow four general behaviors in their communal life (vv. 20-21) and then commands two actions that specifically relate to the crisis (vv. 22-23). He has constructed the exhortations from fundamental features of the Christian faith, making use of two triadic formulas: "faith, hope, and love" and "God, Christ, and the Holy Spirit." The fact that the triplet, "faith, love, and hope" is found frequently in the New Testament (Rom 5:1-5; 1 Cor 13:13; Phil 1:9-10; Col 1:4-5; 1 Thess 1:3; 5:8; 2 Thess 1:3-4; Heb 6:10-12; 10:22-24; 1 Pet 1:3-8) reflects its widespread use in Christian moral catechesis. References to God in conjunction with both Christ and the Holy Spirit occur at Matt 28:19, 1 Cor 12:4-6, Eph 2:18, and 4:4-6.

Jude first calls for the church to engage in "mutual upbuilding." He compares the church to a temple, relying on a metaphor used by many early Christians to describe the community of belief as a dwelling place of God (Eph 2:22, 1 Cor 3:9-15, 1 Pet 2:5). The individual believers have been called into a community founded by Christ's sacrificial death for the sake of others. Therefore they must display the same form of self-sacrifice and love in their treatment of one another. All members are responsible for the community's upkeep: each member must maintain and edify the others, because such actions maintain the unity of the community.

The versatility of the "building" metaphor allowed New Testament writers to adapt it to the needs of their addressees, often identifying the building's foundation with the main tenets of their exhortations (1 Cor 3:9-17, Eph 3:20-22). Jude refers to the foundation as "your most holy faith," by which he means the received gospel message (v. 3). Thus, in contrast to the intruders who rely on themselves and their corrupted understanding of God's grace (v. 4), creating schisms in the church (v. 19), the believing community is built upon the truth that comes from God, and their adherence to the gospel secures the church's unity.

Jude next exhorts the congregation "to pray in the Holy Spirit," which creates a second contrast. The intruders are "worldly people" who do not possess the Spirit (v. 19). Jude's hearers, however, are guided by God's Spirit so their prayer is sincere and genuine. Jude's language suggests communal prayer that is under the control of the Spirit and thus prayer that is faithful to God's will (see also Rom 8:26-27; 1 Cor 12:3; Rom. 8:16-17).

The third injunction (v. 21) urges the congregation "to keep itself in the love of God." The exhortation in verse 21 presupposes God's prior acts (v. 1) and calls for behavior that demonstrates acceptance of God's love and favor. The necessity of this reciprocal action has been displayed through Jude's negative examples in verses 5-7 (especially v. 6, where the term "kept" is used). Israel, the angels, and the inhabitants of Sodom and Gomorrah did not remain in the station appointed to them, and forfeited their place with God. Similarly, the intruders violate their place and thus deny the love of God. Jude's readers, however, should live as a people loved by God, following the precepts and established designs of God. In one sense, the third injunction repeats the first: to keep themselves in the love of God is to act in love toward fellow believers. In another, it repeats the second, for to remain in the love of God is to follow the truth of God and respond to it by the Spirit.

A fourth admonition calls for trust in the promise of God's redemption. "To look forward to the mercy of our Lord Jesus Christ that leads to eternal life" does not mean simply hoping that something might happen, but living with the certainty that an event will occur. "Waiting" in New Testament literature refers to living in full expectation of the *eschaton* (e.g., Rom 8:23; Gal 5:5; Phil 3:20) when the redemption of humanity and creation will occur.

◊   ◊   ◊   ◊

These four exhortations are interrelated. Faithful expectation of Christ's mercy entails proper love toward God's people (Matt

25:45-51), maintenance of God's household (1 Cor 3:16-17; 1 Pet 4:7-11), and reliance upon the Spirit. Likewise, participating in these actions manifests a life of faithful expectation. Believers live in the present toward the future, and this faithful anticipation guarantees eternal life with God.

Specific Commands (22-23)

In verses 22-23, Jude addresses the treatment of community members affected by the intruders. The broad sense of these verses can be understood, but their translation is extremely difficult, because Jude 22-23 is "undoubtedly one of the most [textually] corrupt passages in New Testament literature" (Osburn 1972, 42). Commentators agree only that it "is probably impossible to reach an assured conclusion as to the original text" (Bauckham 1983, 108). Even when a likely "original" reading seems plausible, the language and syntax remain uncertain.

Two basic forms of verses 22-23 are found in the text traditions: a two-clause and a three-clause option. The NRSV follows the longer text contained in the major manuscripts such as Vaticanus and Sinaiticus: "And have mercy on some who are wavering; save others by snatching them out of the fire; and have mercy on still others with fear." The shorter version, which is found in the third-century papyrus manuscript P[72], reads: "Snatch some from the fire; on those who doubt have mercy with fear."

Although no final word is possible, there are good reasons for preferring the shorter reading: it has ancient and widespread support throughout the manuscript traditions; it fits Jude's context; and the longer readings can be explained as expansions and clarifications of the shorter text. Thus, the longer rendering in the NRSV probably should not be accepted (for a full discussion of the difficulties see Osburn 1972, 139-144; Winter 1994, 215-222).

Jude's admonitions in these verses do not refer to the opponents but to two other groups in the congregation. The first group contains those who vacillate between the truth of the gospel and the corrupt teaching of the intruders. They are not quite consumed, but they are "in the fire" (which surely represents hell and judgment for Jude) and on the brink of destruction. Those who have remained obedient must snatch them back from the danger.

Jude also has a second group in view, but how one defines it depends on how the term *diakrinomenos* ("those who doubt/ waver") is understood. When Jude used the term to describe the argument between Michael and the Devil (v. 9), it had the meaning "dispute." If that meaning applies here, then the second group disputes Jude's rebuke of the opposition and must be confronted (see Bauckham 1983, 115). It appears more likely, however, that we should translate *diakrinomenos* as "those who doubt or waver." On this reading, Jude is referring to people who, while attracted to the opposition, are *less* persuaded by them than the first group. Their situation is not as perilous and they do not need to be "snatched back," but forgiven and reasoned with (treated with "mercy in fear"). Since it is only by God's mercy that all the believers will be redeemed, humility and reverence are required. As people who themselves need mercy, they can do nothing other than extend it to their fellow believers. Nevertheless, this must be done "in fear/reverence," respecting both the potency of the opposition and the even more awesome power of God.

Finally, Jude warns the congregation to "hate even the tunic defiled by their bodies." The term "defile" is always used figuratively in early Christian literature (BDAG, 938). Jude means for the congregation to treat this matter with utmost seriousness, since the verb "hating" implies an aversion to and a distinct choice against something (BDAG, 652). A "tunic" is the garment worn next to the skin; Jude's use of it here indicates the depth of the defiling influence, i.e., that certain persons have been contaminated completely and should be placed in "spiritual quarantine." Early Christian communities practiced a form of excommunication whenever one of their members persisted in defective belief or behavior injurious to the community (Matt 18:17, 1 Cor 5:11, 2 John 10-11). Isolating and shunning the offender protected the community from further damage, and prompted the offender to repent and return (1 Cor 5:5). This interpretation fits the context of the letter and follows the patterns of the admonitions in verses 22-23. The congregation must bring those affected by the opposition back to the truth (Jas 5:19-20), even if this requires temporarily avoiding social contact with them (for other interpretations see Neyrey 1993, 92; Winter 1994, 218-219).

CONCLUDING DOXOLOGY (24-25)

Most New Testament letters conclude with a benediction, (e.g., Rom 16:25-27; 1 Cor 16:23-24; 2 Cor 13:14; Gal 6:18; Eph 6:23-24), which is sometimes joined to farewell greetings sent to the church (e.g., Rom 16; 1 Cor 16:19-20; 2 Cor 13:11-13; Phil 4:21-22). Jude has replaced the conventional forms with a doxology, which functions to bid farewell, praise God, and appeal to the congregation's faith in God. By means of its language and thought the doxology forms an inclusion with the letter's prescript. The lack of a benediction and the lack of personal greetings are consonant with Jude's terse intensity; the crisis that precipitated the letter has not passed, though it can now be clearly seen. As Kelly notes, Jude has formulated an "eloquent, liturgical-sounding doxology which at the same time enshrines an aptly phrased prayer for the ultimate welfare of the recipients" (1981, 290).

◊ ◊ ◊ ◊

Doxologies occur elsewhere in the New Testament (e.g., Rom 11:36, 16:25-27; Eph 3:20-21; 1 Thess 5:23; 1 Pet 5:11; 2 Pet 3:18). Typically they have four parts: (1) an address, (2) a word of praise, (3) an indication of time, and (4) "amen." Jude's incorporates all of these, but he has greatly expanded the first and second parts to serve his overall purpose. The doxology first mentions those attributes that reveal God's ability to keep the addressees safe. Here, the verb *tēreō* (v. 1) is not replaced but is balanced by the verb *phylassō* ("guard") in order to emphasize God's constant protection of the believers. The doxology thus contrasts the present believers whom God has called through Christ with the earlier "called ones," who failed due to their lack of trust in God (vv. 5-7).

Unlike those who rebelled, the believers must trust in God, who will preserve them "without falling." This rare adjective refers to God's ability to keep believers from the snares of foes and the perils of life, in particular from the intruders' deceptions that lead to the destruction of the community and the forfeit of salvation. Unlike the unstable opposition (v. 13), whose presence is a source of stumbling and wreckage (v. 12), God is constant and faithful, and therefore trustworthy to keep them from falling.

Jude also wishes for God to bring the believers into the heavenly presence "without blemish" and "with rejoicing." Both of these expressions typically refer to the worship of God. The first recalls Israel's sacrifices in which only animals without defect/blemish were offered in worship (Exod 29:1, Lev 3:1). The second reflects the communal celebration of God's glory as deliverer and redeemer (Isa 12:6; Ps 100). The idea of an unblemished sacrifice was naturally applied to the life of the believer, but Jude also identifies this characteristic as the quality of eschatological heavenly worshippers (see also Eph 5:27; Col 1:22; 1 Thess 3:13). God is holy and without blemish, thus only holy persons may enter God's presence.

The doxology and the letter end with an elaborate recounting of God's saving attributes. God is proclaimed as the one who transcends time, whose authority knows no bounds, and whose sphere of power has no limits. God is "the only God our Savior, through Jesus Christ our Lord." Jude follows early Christian tradition with the appellation "only God," a concept inherited from Judaism. God is understood by Israel as the only true God (Exod 20:2; Deut 6:4; Ps 82:19), and early Christian communities incorporated this confession into their belief and worship (Rom 16:27; 1 Tim 1:17, 6:15-16).

Following the traditional Jewish formulation, God is also referred to as "savior." God is the author and provider of salvation, either of Israel, the church, or an individual in distress (e.g., Deut 32:15; Isa 17:10, Pss 18:1-2, 25:5, 64:7-10). Explicit references to God as Savior are rare in the New Testament (only Luke 1:47; 1 Tim 1:1, 2:3, 4:10; Titus 1:3, 2:10, 3:4); the term typically is transferred to the Christ. Since Christ is God's eschatological agent, the rescue or deliverance is ultimate. Jude is thus referring again to God's ability and desire to deliver believers from destruction and provide them eternal life (see v. 21).

The phrase "through Jesus Christ our Lord" can be connected syntactically either with "our Savior" or with the attributes that follow. The first construction yields the sense that God effects salvation through Christ, and is in keeping with other New Testament formulations (e.g., 2 Cor 5:18, Col 1:20, 1 Tim 2:5). This construction, however, requires an attachment of the preposition "through" to the noun "Savior," which is very rare and strains the Greek grammar. The second option, on the other hand, "glory, power," etc., "be to God through Christ" is found in most other New Testament doxologies (e.g., Rom 16:27, 2 Cor 1:20, 1 Pet 4:11). This option is the likely construction, and suggests that the believing community acknowledges that God receives all glory, majesty, power, and authority through the agency and mediation of Christ.

The doxology mentions four attributes of God. The first, "glory" *(doxa)*, occurs frequently in New Testament doxologies and connotes the radiant nature of God's being. Christians recognize that they have experienced the glory of God through the redemptive power of the resurrection of Jesus from the dead. As a sign of this recognition they acclaim God's glory and power as sufficient for all time.

The remaining attributes stress God's transcendence: God's majesty, power, and authority. Individually, the attributes refer to the extent of God's power, but conjoined they break through the imagination and point to a reality beyond language. Their rhetorical impact comes from their concatenation. The Greek term for "majesty" occurs in other doxologies (e.g., 1 Chron 29:11; *1 Clem* 20:12), and it is used only of God in the Bible. It reflects the greatness of God, both in power (*1 Clem* 16:2) and in speech (*1 Clem* 27:4). Jude enhances this idea by the accompanying attribute, "power," also typical of doxologies (1 Tim 6:16;

2 Pet 4:11), which describes God's might, strength, and dynamism. The doxology then acclaims God's "authority" as a force that brokers no opposition and asserts God's sovereign freedom to act (BDAG, 352-353).

The doxology ends with a triple reference to time that expresses God's temporal transcendence: "before all time and now and forever." This phrase forms a parallel with the previous attributes. Just as God transcends all descriptions and attributions, no matter how grand, so God is beyond time. Through all space, beyond all time, God exists as the all in all. It is this constant, eternal reality of God that guarantees the truth of God's being and love. The doxology concludes with "amen," literally "it is so." When the letter was read, the congregation joined in pronouncing "amen," thus acknowledging the truth of Jude's claims. In this communal "amen" they announce with him that they are ready to contend for the "faith that has been entrusted to them once for all" (Bauckham 1983, 115).

◊ ◊ ◊ ◊

The final exhortations and doxology reiterate Jude's two fundamental themes: the complete integration of belief with actions and the necessity of fidelity to God's purposes. The concluding doxology emphasizes God's saving actions through Christ as well as God's sovereignty. These realities undergird the exhortations in verses 20-22. Because God is holy, those who claim allegiance to God must respond in holiness—not because they are compelled to find God's favor, but rather because they understand and respect God's nature (e.g., 1 Pet 1:15). The merciful one expects that those who have received favor will show it to others—hence Jude's admonition to "have mercy on those who are wavering." Though this is a strong letter, stark and unyielding, it is nevertheless based on the realization that God has acted to redeem humanity. It is not a surprise then that those who denigrate or attempt to hinder that redemption will receive God's disfavor. On the other hand, those who remain true to that purpose will be sustained by God and "join in the presence of his glory with rejoicing."

INTRODUCTION: 2 PETER

L ike Jude, 2 Peter has not enjoyed a favored status in the church or with biblical interpreters. This appears to have plagued the letter almost from its inception. Existing patristic evidence suggests that the letter was rarely used or quoted in the second and third centuries. It is not among the documents listed in the Muratorian Canon (an early list of books considered to be scripture), and Origen (ca. 185–351 CE), who seems to have known the letter, doubted its authenticity (Eusebius, *Hist. Eccl.* 6.25.11). Eusebius placed the epistle under the category of *Antilegomena* ("disputed books"), because while he thought that 2 Peter had some use, it did not appear to him qualified for canonical status.

In more modern periods, the letter has fared no better. Indeed, as John Elliott notes, "Down to the present day its canonical status and theological significance seem to have remained more a theory than a fact" (Elliott 1982, 119). As a result, outside of a few pithy maxims—the infamous "dogs returning to their vomit" and the dictum "to the Lord one day is as a thousand years and a thousand years as a day,"—it is a writing rarely quoted or studied. A few passages from 2 Peter appear in the lectionary, but sermons developed from them are rare, and the letter has not been a staple of New Testament preaching or studies.

Even so, both the community of belief and the community of New Testament scholars can benefit from a fresh consideration of 2 Peter. First, it can provide a valuable window onto the struggles of the nascent church, which any complete portrait of early Christianity should include. Second, the letter invites its readers to consider the intellectual demands and moral components of belief and fidelity. Finally, even if the author could be excessive in his manner of writing and degree of denunciation, we can emulate his passion for truth and his commitment to his readers.

PLACE AND TIME

Any attempt to assign a date to 2 Peter or to establish its place of origin must remain speculative. It is likely that its author incorporated large sections of Jude into his work and since Jude was probably written in the late first century, 2 Peter could not have been written any earlier. Internal evidence supports this, especially the letter's notation that the apostolic generation had passed away (3:4). The reference to a collection of Paul's letters (3:15-16), which would not have started until 75–80 CE, provides further evidence of a later rather than earlier composition. Further, the letter's style and language (as well as some of its concerns) bear resemblance to *1 Clement* and the *Shepherd of Hermas*, both written in the second century. Since there are clear references to the letter in the *Apocalypse of Peter* (ca. 135–140 CE), the upper range for the composition date must be no later than 115–120 CE. An educated guess might place the letter somewhere between 90 and 100 CE.

The letter's origin and destination are even less certain than its date. Still, 2 Peter does address actual problems and the letter certainly was sent to a specific church or group of churches. Unfortunately, their identity cannot be determined because instead of a standard opening address, the author begins with a generic reference to "those who have received a faith as precious as ours." And, instead of sending final greetings to specific members of the congregation, the author closed the letter with a benediction and a doxology. Nevertheless, the references to the audience as "the beloved" (1:17; 3:1, 8, 14), and the note that it had received letters from Paul (3:15), along with their identification as converts (3:2) suggest that the letter was addressed to an actual congregation.

Some scholars suggest an Egyptian origin or address since *The*

Apocalypse of Peter was also from that region. Others, referring to internal evidence, such as the ascription of the letter to Peter and the reference to Paul's letters, suggest Rome as a possibility. Still others, arguing that 3:1 refers to 1 Peter, suggest Asia Minor (see 1 Pet 1:1). Given the author's heavy use of Jewish-Hellenistic terminology, his rhetorical style, and the similarity of the "opposition's" arguments to Epicurean philosophy, almost any Greek speaking congregation in Asia or Egypt could qualify as a candidate.

FORM AND CONTENT

Second Peter is best understood as a document of polemical defense and moral exhortation. On the one hand, its author responds to teaching that challenged belief in God's providence and the reality of a future judgment (1:16-21; 3:5-11) with denouncements of the people who brought the teaching (2:12, 17-18). On the other hand, admonitions to the audience to live righteously while it waits for the day of judgment and salvation (1:5-11; 3:11-13, 14-15) are interspersed among the author's critiques and ripostes.

Although it seems to open with a partial epistolary prescript, there is little in the rest of 2 Peter that follows standard Greek letters. In fact, the actual content of the document, particularly its warnings and exhortations, is typically found in another ancient literary convention—the "farewell testament." By framing a "farewell testament" within features of an ancient letter, the author of 2 Peter created a novel form, with no real analogies either in the New Testament or ancient Jewish/Christian literature.

Examples of the "farewell testament," however, are found in both the New and Old Testaments as well as in later "Christian" material. The testaments of Jacob (Gen 49), Moses (Deut 31-33), and Joshua (Josh 23-24) illustrate its significance for the tradition of Israel. The New Testament depicts both Jesus (Luke 22:14-36; John 13-17) and Paul (Acts 20:17-35) addressing their disciples before death, warning them of future hardships, and offering instructions for a life of faith.

Typically "farewell testaments" are pseudepigraphic, since by attributing the advice they contain to a seminal or founding figure of renown, an author endows it with an authority well beyond his own. The particular instances of the form vary depending on the author's aim, so standard elements of the genre cannot be established firmly (see Neyrey 1993, 163). However, examples like *The Testaments of the Twelve Patriarchs* show that a farewell discourse usually contained five key elements.

1. The leader, aware of his imminent death, gathers his followers or family.

2. Often he recounts details about his life and reminds the group of its heritage and history.

3. The leader admonishes the audience to cultivate particular virtues and to avoid forms of vice or inappropriate behavior.

4. The exhortation often culminates in a charge to live according to the "law of the Lord" or in obedience to God's commands.

5. This charge is often accompanied by a warning of evil to come, either from outside forces or from members of the group who have disobeyed the truth.

Second Peter contains four of the elements of the farewell testament. Chapter 1 refers to Peter's imminent death (1:12-14) and his earlier life experiences (1:16-19). Chapters 1 and 3 provide the moral exhortations, and warnings of future crises occur in 2:1-3 and 3:1-7.

By their nature, farewell testaments are fictional, i.e., they are written after the events they "predict," but are presented as if those events had not yet occurred. In such discourses, a family patriarch or community founder addressed a community to prepare it for the challenges of impostors that would inevitably follow his departure or death. Admonitions to remain faithful to the original teachings and to practice an irreproachable morality also typified the remarks.

In the case of 2 Peter, it is evident that the "predicted" false teachers had already joined the congregation before the letter was written (see 2:17-19, 3:4-5). Since it is unlikely that the letter's actual author had sufficient credentials or social status to challenge the opposition, he constructed a "farewell testament" attributed to the apostle Peter in order to present and authorize his own arguments against them as those of the prestigious apostle Peter. As Peter's last testament, the arguments and admonitions of the letter could be portrayed as trustworthy representations of historical fact. As a result of his rhetorical strategy, the author increased his chances of exposing his opponents' errors and gaining the acceptance of his own positions.

Invoking the authority of the apostle Peter also enabled him to demonstrate that the teaching of the opposition departed from God's truth (1:16-18), and that following it would lead the unsuspecting believers to moral destruction (2:15, 18, 19, 20-21). The author understood that pragmatic re-formulations of the Christian faith were necessary for the church to thrive in a changing world. He also realized that certain castings of the Christian message could result in dissolution of the faith and lead to social assimilation if proper boundaries were not maintained. He believed that the other teachers had exceeded those boundaries and that, in their efforts to make Christian belief more comprehensible, they had compromised its integrity. He wrote in order to re-establish the boundaries between truth and falsehood, to expose the other teachers as apostates (2:20-21), and to call the community back to its initial belief and piety.

AUTHORSHIP AND LITERARY STYLE

The fictive "farewell testament" suggests that 2 Peter is pseudonymous, as acknowledged by almost every modern New

Testament scholar. There are good reasons for this position. First, even though its author seems to refer to 1 Peter (3:1, see comment), outside of a general concern for eschatology and a call to ethical living, there is virtually no intersection between the content of 2 Peter and 1 Peter. Second, while both were written under Peter's name, the two epistles display radically different styles and language. First Peter tends toward a straightforward and clear syntax and its vocabulary, while context specific, is neither rare nor ornate. Second Peter is written in a grandiose style with ornate use of figures and its language is far removed from everyday use (alternatively considered pretentious [Johnson 1999, 496] or typical of an Asiatic style given to excess [Neyrey 1993, 119-120]).

The ambitious techniques of the author include his use of alliteration, assonance, and repetition. The author frequently creates synonymous pairs, conjoining nouns and adjectives to amplify his thought (1:3, 4, 8, 9, 10, 16, 17; 2:10, 11, 13; 3:7, 11, 14, 16). The author is also fond of unusual phrasing and unique words. Of the 401 different words used in this letter, 57 appear nowhere else in the New Testament, and 38 more occur only once or twice in the rest of the New Testament material. Even more remarkable, 32 of 2 Peter's terms appear nowhere else in the entire Greek Bible. Of these, 15 occur in Jewish-Hellenistic literature, but 11 are rarely found in any ancient Greek literature.

The style and language of the document reveal that 2 Peter's closest literary and intellectual relatives are early second-century materials from Hellenistic Judaism, and the Christian documents the *Shepherd of Hermas*, and *1* and *2 Clement*. Just as these writings interpreted earlier tradition in the light of Greek and Roman cultural expectations, 2 Peter adopted an abundance of Hellenistic terms and figures to explicate early Christianity's traditions. Beliefs such as the interaction of God with nature and the return of Christ for cosmic judgment, which had their roots in Judaism, are "translated" into the vernacular of the Gentile converts that made up his audience.

NATURE OF THE OPPOSITION

The repetitive style and unusual vocabulary reveal the urgency of the author's warnings about the opposition and the disaster that following them would bring. We should note that the author seemingly never intended to provide an objective description of his opponents, and his trenchant use of vivid metaphors and figures of speech paints unflattering portraits of them. From his perspective, the other teachers were a menace for his audience and he did not consider it his task to present them dispassionately. Rather, they needed to be exposed and ultimately made to depart. Hence, his is not an objective presentation but a polemical one, constructed to refute and disparage. This limits any hypothetical sketch of the opponents or the positions they took. Fortunately, because the audience knew these teachers, the author could not completely misrepresent them or his own counter-arguments would have lost credibility. Hence, the letter does provide some sense of the opposition's ideas.

It is quite likely that the other teachers did not (at least originally) consider themselves as opponents, but simply interpreters of the gospel who were intent on articulating the elements of Christian belief. They, like other early Christians, believed that Christian convictions and expressions, rooted in Jewish belief structure, had to be modified for non-Jewish audiences if the faith were to remain viable. Thus, far from ignoring true doctrine as the author suggested, they would have understood themselves as clarifying and enhancing it.

The opposition appears to have held four basic ideas. First, the future return of Christ as cosmic judge was not a genuine part of Christian teaching, but a fabricated myth (1:16-21). Second, it was impossible to continue in this belief since the "promises" on which it was based had not been fulfilled (3:8-10). Third, because God does not intervene in the course of human affairs, there would be no future judgment of humans for their conduct. In fact, such actions would be contrary to divine will and intent (3:5-7). Finally, either because God had already forgiven the sins of Christians or because there would be no future judgment, human beings should determine their own moral codes and conduct (2:19).

This construction of the opposition's ideas suggests a close resemblance to stock depictions of Epicurean belief (see Neyrey, 122-127). Based on their understanding of the universe and their focus on human agency, Epicureans denied the involvement of the deity in human history. Moreover, since the cosmos was only a series of chance occurrences, predictions about its future course could not be made in any rational manner. Since Epicureans did not envision an existence after death, they rejected any notion of a post-mortem judgment of the wicked or the just. Epicureans held that at best, such ideas were merely mythical devices for manipulating the conduct of an undereducated public. However, by properly instructing the public, these myths could become dispensable.

By the time 2 Peter was written, Epicurean conceptions had been popularized sufficiently enough that they were no longer distinctly "Epicurean." In fact, the other teachers likely were not Epicureans, but had adopted some of their epistemological tenets and applied them to the Christian faith.

Not surprisingly, Epicurean thought provoked responses from other philosophical schools, including caricatures of their positions. The Epicurean idea that one should seek pleasure typically was construed as a desire for immorality or debauchery. Likewise, the denial of a provident deity was characterized as atheism. Our author has used these stock depictions against his opponents. He imputes to them the most offensive and immoral of motives for their activity, and charges them with obtuse stubbornness. They are characterized as "pseudo-prophets," who deny Christ as Master (2:1) and who, in their ignorance will slander the divine beings (2:10). They are blemishes on the congregation (2:13) who speak "bombastic nonsense" and are destined for a destruction they have brought on themselves (2:1, 3).

RELATIONSHIP TO JUDE

While there is almost no example of identical wording in Jude and 2 Peter, the linguistic correspondences between them are too numerous to be explained by coincidence. The following table illustrates the parallel passages:

Comparable passages in Jude and 2 Peter

Jude	2 Peter
4	2:1-2
5	2:3
6	2:4
7	2:6
8	2:10
9	2:11
10	2:12
11	2:13-16
12	2:13, 17
13	2:17
16	2:18
17	3:1-2
18	3:3

The connections between Jude 4-16 and 2 Pet 2:1-18 are unmistakable, and only some form of literary dependence can explain the high degree of overlap. Four options are possible: (1) 2 Peter was the source for Jude, (2) Jude was the source for 2 Peter, (3) both used a common source, or (4) one person authored both letters.

The fourth option is not tenable because the differences in authorial style make it impossible to consider that the letters come from the same hand. Further, the imagery common to both letters is used in markedly different ways and for different purposes (e.g., Jude 13 compared to 2 Pet 2:17). The possibility that there was a single source for both letters can account for the fact that while there are numerous affinities, actual verbal agreement between Jude and 2 Peter is rare. However, no common source has been discovered, and there is no ancient evidence for its existence. Moreover, hypothetical constructions of the source yield something almost identical to Jude itself. If the common source did exist, one is hard-pressed to explain why Jude would have been composed.

The early church adopted the idea that Jude used 2 Peter; this position is still held by a few modern scholars (e.g., Mayor, 1965). Ancient interpreters probably presumed that a lesser figure (Jude) would borrow from a well-known one (Peter) rather than for the reverse to occur. Modern arguments for this position are robust, but there are three significant reasons for not accepting them. First, since the apostle Peter did not write the letter, the idea that its author would not copy from Jude is rendered moot. Second, Jude 4-16 is a carefully structured literary unit, but its counterparts in 2 Peter appear in a piecemeal fashion. This suggests that the author of 2 Peter selected his material from Jude's balanced figures rather than that Jude formed 2 Peter's ad hoc sentences into a tight rhetorical structure. Third, it is more plausible to understand 2 Peter as an expansion of Jude than to consider Jude as a reduction of 2 Peter. Thus, it is more likely that the author of 2 Peter incorporated Jude's letter into his polemic than that Jude refashioned 2 Peter.

The commentary shows that while Jude served as a source for 2 Peter, the author added, edited, and, on occasion, omitted material from that letter as his own argument required (3:3). Jude's judgments of the disobedient appealed to the author of 2 Peter as he compiled his indictments of the other teachers. He used Jude mostly for the character arguments mounted in chapter 2, though he did borrow and refit that letter for other purposes also (cf. Jude 17, 2 Pet 3:2; cf. Jude 18, 2 Pet 3:3).

The most striking variations are the modifications of Jude's readings of Old Testament texts (Jude 6-7; 8-12) and the omission of his quotation from *1 Enoch* (Jude 14-15). The author of 2 Peter likely refashioned Jude's examples from *1 Enoch* and *The Testament of Moses,* because they were obscure to his audience or because they were too similar to the myths he had denied using (1:16). It is also possible that the author had a restricted understanding of which texts could be considered authoritative, so he omitted any that might have been suspect or speculative (Kelly 1981, 227). In the final analysis, while the two letters share much in common, their purposes, forms of arguments, and opponents differ significantly. As a result, each letter should be interpreted in its own right.

THEOLOGY AND PURPOSE

One interpreter has argued that almost every significant and interesting idea in early Christian thought, from the nature of the apostolic office to the conception of God's eschaton, has been blunted or changed for the worse by the author of this epistle (Käsemann 1982, 177). One can take issue with this assessment, while also admitting that the letter's theology is not particularly daring, and that its approach toward belief in God and Christ tends toward a conservation of the past. However, 2 Peter was not constructed as a piece of theology, and its critics make a mistake when they it evaluate it on that ground. Our author sought other goals. He was engaged in refutation and wanted to remind his audience of the need to hold firm to their foundational beliefs. His letter is itself an argument against particular innovations of Christian beliefs that he considered detrimental to his congregation. The letter is best understood as an exercise in proper adaptation and interpretation of the Christian faith.

The opponents apparently proposed that certain fundamentals of the faith would have to be refashioned or rejected if Christianity were to remain practicable. They also suggested that a renovation of eschatological belief would entail revising the moral commitments required of God's people. The author of 2 Peter, while admitting to the necessity of adaptation and translation of Christian belief into a common vernacular, opposed the premises and manner of his opponents' reformulation of Christian tradition.

Three argumentative thrusts are maintained throughout the

epistle. First, the author insists that a relationship with God requires trust in God and a life conducted with ethical integrity (1:5-11; 3:9). Second, this relationship will be validated when God's public intervention in history takes place. At that time those who refused God's overtures will be condemned to remain alienated from God, while those who lived according to God's desires will be accepted into eternal existence with God (1:9, 11; 2:9-10). Third, whether one consulted God's written word, God's prophets, or God's most recent agents (the apostles), one would find a consonance between their teaching and the author's understanding of the gospel. This was especially true with respect to God's established pattern of interactions with and for the world, including Christ's return as cosmic judge. Thus, despite his opponents' claims that the second coming could not be maintained as really occurring, the author insisted that Christ would appear at the end of time and would hold a universal accounting.

Second Peter's author attempted to respond to the challenges that arise when received beliefs no longer appear tenable and when societal expectations suggest that they should be abandoned. In particular, those challenges revolved around human freedom and responsibility and God's provenance and interaction with contemporary history. Every vital community of faith, or at least every community of faith that desires to be vital, faces similar challenges. To meet them, these communities must enter into an exercise of reformulation. Second Peter can serve as an important model for such deliberations. Three traits of the letter suggest as much. First, its author understood that the Church exists as God's people only if it is continually oriented by its fundamental traditions. Second, the author knew that the Church could not release its eschatological moorings if it wished to understand God's actions in the world. Third, the author insisted that what one believes affects how one acts, and how one lives is an indication of what one believes. Second Peter is a model for the Church's deliberations because it shows a genuine encounter with the past while simultaneously holding that valid reinterpretation of tradition will not release the church from its moral responsibilities.

We do not know if the author succeeded, but even if his attempts failed, the contemporary church can admire and learn from these efforts. If we read 2 Peter seriously, we will recognize why attempts to translate difficult beliefs responsibly are crucial to the church's intellectual and spiritual integrity. We will also be reminded that in this exercise of reformulation, God's purposes can never be constrained or denied by efforts of the human intellect. The opposition did not err in providing translations of the ancient traditions, but by presuming to place limits on how and when God could act. The author of 2 Peter recognized this as a denial of God's sovereignty. Hence, while he admonished his readers to engage in their own reformulations, he also reminded them to maintain a proper reverence for God.

Second Peter's reformulation of early eschatological belief may appear archaic today, but it continues to pose a challenge to the contemporary church. This letter insists that the church be involved in thoughtful exercises of re-interpretation, which acknowledge the past while accommodating the present. Second Peter's reformulations can also serve as a catalyst for the church and a scale by which to judge its own attempts to comprehend and make intelligible the faith we have received (1:1).

COMMENTARY: 2 PETER

PRESCRIPT (1:1-2)

Second Peter begins with a conventional epistolary prescript: "From sender to addressees, greetings" (see comments on Jude 1). Like most New Testament letter writers, the author has adapted the formula to his needs and argumentative goals. A comparison to 1 Peter makes clear the degree of adaptation. The author of 1 Peter refers to himself simply as "Peter, an apostle of Jesus Christ," while our author uses the more detailed description, "Symeon Peter, a servant and apostle of Jesus Christ." The addition of the Semitic name (*Symeon*) and the designation "servant and apostle" present a particular view of the author. Because other teachers had entered the community and achieved a degree of success, the author felt compelled to refute their teaching, which he considered false doctrine (see 2:1-3, 20-22; 3:3-7; see introduction). To accomplish this goal, he first had to establish authoritative credentials. By adopting Peter's mantle, he differentiates himself from his opponents and claims an apostolic authority they do not possess.

The double name "Simon Peter" is not unique (almost 50 times in the New Testament) but the use of the Hebraic form *Symeon* is. Acts employs this form to refer to Peter at the Jerusalem Council (Acts 15:14), and in that context the Semitic form is natural. Why our author uses it is not so obvious. Since the letter is pseudonymous, the Semitic form is probably used to establish that the author is writing under the aegis of the apostle Peter known originally as *Symeon bar Jonah*. By claiming apostolic identity, the author presents himself as one of the original and most intimate of Christ's disciples (Mark 3:14; Matt 16:18, John 21:15-17), and lends authority to his arguments.

The self-identification continues with a reference to "servant" (see comment on Jude 1) and "apostle." It is not unusual to find this dual designation in a prescript (Rom 1:1; Titus 1:1), especially when it serves a legitimating function. The terms highlight different facets of Peter's status. As an "apostle," the author assumes the role of authorized spokesperson and delegate of Christ. As servant, the author is pledged to follow the rule of Christ. Thus the audience can trust that as Christ's servant and apostle, "Peter" will provide the unadulterated message of Christ's teaching.

In contrast to his expanded self-description, the author provides only a minimal description of the audience. A typical prescript often refers to the audience's geographic location or its relationship to other congregations (e.g., 1 Cor 1:2; Gal 1:1, see comment on Jude 1). In place of the typical geographic detail, however, our author has supplied a statement about the gospel message and its enduring value. He writes to *tois isotimon hēmin lachousin* (either "those who have equal standing in Christ" or "those who have received a faith as precious as ours," NRSV). By referring to his audience in this more general fashion, the author widens the scope of the letter to all believers, regardless of their locale. This open message contrasts to the opposition whose teaching was reserved for a privileged few and who "secretly bring in destructive opinions" (2:1). The author, on the other hand, shows that he remains true to the fundamental gospel, which has not changed (see also 1:10-11, 12-13).

The author here uses the term "faith" for the content and teaching of Christian belief, rather than the volitional act of trust (see Jude 3). He compares the value of the recipients' faith with "ours," by which he means the faith of the apostles. Since the gospel has been made available to all, in equal measure, there is no difference between the truths provided to the initial hearers and the truth taught to those who came later, as the term *isotimon* confirms. The NRSV translation, "as precious as," while technically accurate, can be misleading because it emphasizes only one aspect of the term, i.e., equality in value. The word also suggests equality in kind, i.e., "of the same nature or content." The author wants to assure the audience that it possesses exactly the same doctrine and knowledge as the apostles. By referring to their faith as *isotimon*, the author assures them that they have the same gospel and therefore, the same benefits and redeemed status that the first believers had.

By the same token, the addressees must display the same fidelity the apostles showed (Elliott, 1982, 134). The value of "the faith" is based in God's will and desire, which guarantees that the gospel teaching is never incomplete or defective, and shows that the gospel message is not to be disobeyed or changed. Later generations of believers are at no disadvantage because the message they have received carries the benefits and privileges equal to those of the first believers. Therefore, they are also responsible for living in a manner consonant with those privileges.

The substantive participle "those who have received" typically was used for the act of obtaining something, often by divine will (BDAG, 581). By employing it, the author connects the community's existence to God's will and desire (see 1:3, 10). Since God's beneficence founded and sustained the community, its place in God's plan is secure. This focus on God as the sufficient provider for every believer's needs continues throughout the letter (1:3, 4, 8, 11; 2:9; 3:9).

The author's reference to God's "righteousness" also highlights God's initiative. Terms for "righteousness" occur seven times in the letter (1:1, 13; 2:5, 7, 8, 21; 3:13), demonstrating their importance. The phrase "through the righteousness of our God and Savior Jesus Christ" locates the validity of the faith in God's character rather than in human endeavor, and thus emphasizes God's equal treatment of all. The author's use of "righteousness of God" does not carry the meaning of God's fidelity to and justifying actions toward the world (cf. Rom 1:17, 3:21), as it often does in Paul's letters, but focuses on a more basic meaning of righteousness: the notion of fairness and just action. No one is privileged above others in matters of divine redemption. All have equal standing before God.

The title "Savior" is rarely applied to Christ in the New Testatment, so it is remarkable that five of these instances are in 2 Peter (1:1, 11; 2:20; 3:2, 18). Both Jewish and Christian writings employed the term to describe God's saving actions (see comment on Jude 25), and it was often used in the Hellenistic world to refer to beneficent gods or the Roman emperor (Foerster 1971, 1004-1112). New Testament writers rarely use the word, perhaps because they wanted to distinguish their religion from other forms of Greco-Roman piety. In contrast, the author of 2 Peter uses it precisely because it had this connotation among non-Jews and is a "sign of his willingness to use the religious vocabulary of his Hellenistic environment to communicate the gospel meaningfully to Gentile converts" (Bauckham 1983, 169).

Verse 2 contains a conventional "wish formula" found in both Christian and Jewish letters contemporary with 2 Peter. Following the standard form, our author expresses his desire that God's mercy and peace (in the sense of well being) will characterize the community, but he amplifies the wish formula with language drawn from Jude 2 and perhaps 1 Pet 1:2. The wished-for blessings will occur "through knowledge of God and our Lord Jesus Christ. The NRSV translates the preposition *en* as "in," but the translation "through" or "by" more correctly conveys the author's intent. *Through* knowledge *(epignōsis)* of God and Jesus the blessings will be theirs in abundance.

In 2 Peter, God or Christ is typically the object of *epignōsis* (1:2, 3, 8; 2:20) and the composite phrase [knowledge of God/knowledge of Christ] defines what he regards as essential Christianity (Kelly 1981, 298-299). In Christian teaching, *epignōsis* almost becomes a technical term for knowledge obtained through conversion (Heb 10:26; 1 Tim 2:4; 2 Tim 2:25, 3:7; Titus 1:1). The term is also important for our author, who uses it to designate knowledge that decisively alters one's life (1:3, 8; 2:20). Knowledge of Christ fundamentally changes a believer's lifestyle, shifting not only cognition of facts, but also affecting the very core of self-understanding (Picirelli 1975, 85-93).

◊ ◊ ◊ ◊

The adoption of an apostolic identity provides the first instance of the author's strategy of differentiation (1:16-18; 2:13, 17-21; 3:1-3, 14-18). The self-identification in 1:1 confers on the author the authority and status of the apostle Peter. Since the other teachers could not claim such status, this casts doubt on the validity of their teaching and undermines their claim to present an alternative interpretation of the gospel. In contrast, the author remains true to the fundamental faith established by God and calls the audience to depend on the "knowledge of God/Christ" that they have already experienced.

References to "knowing Christ" are rare elsewhere in the New Testament, but prominent in 2 Peter (1:2, 3, 8; 2:20; 3:18), reflecting the author's concern to show the interaction of the church with Christ, now and in the future. While the author wants his audience to possess knowledge *about* Christ, he is even more concerned that they gain a personal knowledge *of* Christ. In this regard the "knowledge" *(epiginōsis)* of God and Jesus our Lord is functionally equivalent to a faith *(pistis)* equal to ours. The fundamental difference is that *epiginōsis* stresses existential shifts that occur with such knowledge, while *pistis* refers to its contents. In both cases the one who possesses this knowledge or faith recognizes that it not only informs, but also transforms its holder.

BODY OF THE LETTER (1:3–3:16)

Faith and Morality (1:3-11)

The author of 2 Peter had two basic aims: to emphasize faith's ethical component and to counter the detractors who were causing harm and distress. Throughout the letter the two aims are never far from the surface, and they are almost always interrelated. When the author presents examples of faith and moral conduct, he is always mindful of the influence of the opposition. Conversely, when he directs attention to the influence of the opposition, he often points to the deficiency of their character, which reflects an inappropriate understanding of the faith. In verses 1 and 2 the author implied a connection of belief with ethics. In this section he makes the connection explicit.

Verses 1:3-11 constitute 2 Peter's foundational statement of the believer's existence, the core of which is a list of virtues that begins with fidelity and ends with a call for affection and love (vv. 5-7). An initial statement about God's promises of salvation (vv. 3-4) and a concluding promise of eschatological existence with God (vv. 10-11) frame the list. The construction shows that belief manifests itself in righteous behavior, and righteous behavior, in turn, confirms the believers' election. Because the concluding promise affirms the reality of the "eternal kingdom," it also indicts those who denied the future occurrence of the second coming (see 3:3-4, 8-10).

The Call to Christian Existence (1:3-4)

Verses 3 and 4 form one thought unit that modifies the ideas in verse 2 and provides the basis for the exhortation contained in verses 5-7. Since God elects believers by grace (vv. 1-2) and provides them with all they need for a life of faithfulness (vv. 3-4), they should reflect their election (vv. 5-11) in their moral conduct.

◊ ◊ ◊ ◊

Two syntactic features of these verses make them difficult to interpret: the use of the pronoun "his" in verse 3, and the peculiar phrases "life and godliness" and "divine power." Greek grammar would suggest that the pronoun "his" refers to Christ, but in the New Testament it is typically God, not Christ, who calls Christians, and the other terms used in this verse, particularly "glory and goodness" also are usually attributed to God. Thus, it is likely that the author is referring to God's election of believers. Still, the possibility that Christ is the referent in these verses should not be ruled out, and "one is tempted to think that the author has not sorted the matter out clearly in his own mind" (Kelly 1981, 300). If the author was referring to Christ's divine power, he was not suggesting that Christ is a second God, but that Christ shares in God's power. He later makes this point clear, declaring that God transferred "honor and glory" to Christ, which will become manifest at the second coming (1:16-17; cf. Rom 1:4, so Bauckham 1983, 177; Fornberg 1977, 144).

Through "divine power" Christians possess "everything needed for life and godliness." The phrase "divine power" is unique in the New Testament. In fact, this is the only Christian use of the expression prior to Justin (*1 Apol.* 32). Indeed, the use of *theias* ("divine") is rare in the New Testament (only 1:3-4 and Acts 17:29). However, both "divine" and "power" were often used in Greek philosophical discourse, and Hellenistic Jewish writers (e.g., Philo and Josephus) employed the phrase "divine power" to express God's work in the physical realm (see Holladay 1977, 57-66, 177-83).

While the author's phrasing is unusual, his conception of divine power is not. Writers of both the Old and New Testaments regularly acclaimed God's wondrous power and its miraculous manifestations (e.g., Job 27:3; Acts 2:22; Rom 1:16; 13:4). New Testament writers often attribute this power to Christ, especially with regard to the signs and wonders that manifest God's reign (Matt 24:30; Mark 5:30; Luke 5:17; Heb 1:3). That divine power sustains Christians was a standard part of early instruction. The author of 2 Peter, however, expresses this with language drawn from Greek religious thought in order to convey this fundamental feature of Christian teaching in the idiom of the audience's Hellenistic culture.

It is through *epignōsis*, "fundamental knowledge of Christ" (as in v. 2), that the believers "have been given" the means for a "godly life." The author uses the perfect tense of the verb *doreisthai* ("to give"—only three times in the New Testament: here, 1:4 and Mark 15:45) to signify that the "fundamental knowledge" was granted through their conversion and is still in effect. Thus, from the beginning of their Christian existence they have had the ability to live a life of godliness.

One gift God's power bestows is *eusebeia* ("godliness"), a

word that denotes piety toward the gods, especially in terms of proper self-conduct. This word, though rarely used elsewhere in the New Testament, occurs frequently in 2 Peter (1:6; 7; 3:11; see the cognate *eusebōs* in 2:9), suggesting that it is another key element in the letter's argument. It is another term he has adopted from Hellenistic moral writers, to express the correct ethical response to God's sustaining power (see 1 Tim 2:2; 4:7, 8; 6:3, 5, 6 for a similar appropriation of the term).

One of the author's stylistic devices is the use of tandem terms to express a single idea (e.g., 1:3, 4, 8, 9, 10, 16, 17; 2:10, 11, 13; 3:7, 11, 14, 16). The technique is employed three times in verse 4. In the first instance, the words "life" and "godliness" are joined to create the idea of "a life characterized by godliness" (so also "the way of righteousness," in 2:21). The author is contrasting the "godly life" to "the corruption that is in the world because of lust," which he refers to in verse 4.

The author uses a second word pair, "glory and goodness" to underscore the divine initiative for "godliness" and to describe in another way God's "divine power." God's "glorious goodness" grants "godliness" to the readers. Both words occur separately in the verses that follow ("glory" in 1:17 and "goodness" in 1:5), undoubtedly under the influence of this phrase. Here, however, the combination is important, because the resulting image amplifies the earlier descriptions of God's actions.

A third synonymous pair describes God's benefits in verse 4. Divine power not only gives believers the means for a life of piety, but access to God's "precious and very great promises" as well. As in the previous examples, the author employs the word pair to stress the magnitude of God's promises. The repetition of the verb "has given" *(doresthai)* further amplifies this rhetorical effect and stresses the permanence of the promises.

The promises to which the author refers are the coming of Christ and the final transformation of the creation (1:11, 16; and see the use of "promise" elsewhere in the letter: 3:13, 3:4, 9). Through trust in these promises the believers enter the eternal kingdom, described here as "participating in the divine nature" and "escaping from the corruption of the world." Unfortunately, the NRSV translation reverses the Greek word order and treats the aorist participle "escaping" as though it referred to a future possibility ("so that you may escape from the corruption"). In fact, verse 4 refers to God's prior liberating event and is better translated "that you may be partakers of the divine nature since you *have* escaped the corruption of the world" (so Bauckham 1983, 182; Kelly 1981, 302).

While the "corruption that is in the world" can refer to moral decadence (e.g., Gal 6:7), here it more likely refers to the decay or decomposition of nature (see also 1 Cor 15:42, 50; Gal 6:8; 2 Pet 2:12). The affinity between the author's expressions and those of classical Greek philosophy suggests that he is arguing that the entire physical world is temporal and controlled by a process of degeneration (see Bauckham 1983, 182; Fornberg 1977, 88-89; Kelly 1981, 302; Mayor 1965, 177).

The author, like other New Testament writers, affirms that Christians will exchange a transitory (i.e., corruptible) mortal existence for an immortal one at the second coming of Christ (see, e.g., 1 Cor 15:42, 52-54). Taken in isolation, the imagery of verse 4 could suggest a form of body/soul dichotomy, a conception resisted elsewhere in the New Testament (notably 1 Cor 15:42-50). Given the eschatological language elsewhere in the epistle, especially 1:11; 3:13-14, however, it is clear that the author does not conceive of the soul existing separately from the body.

Even though the author focuses primarily on physical decomposition, the moral overtone of "corruption" is not entirely lacking, because the author attributes the corruption in the world to "lust" *(epithymia)*. Whereas Greek philosophy took the world to be corrupted intrinsically, our author understands corruption as a result of aberrant human behavior. For him, death and decay are not natural states, but the result of sin or lust (see Rom 5:12, 8:20-21; Eph 4:22).

The final phrase of verse 4, "and may become participants of the divine nature," is arresting because of its distinctive language and its suggestion that human beings can have divine existence. Like the term "divine," *physis* ("nature") rarely occurs in New

Testament literature (13 times) and only twice with reference to the nature of God (Gal 4:8; Eph 2:3). But to what extent and by what means any human being could participate in the divine nature was a central issue among philosophical and religious thinkers.

Greek philosophers held that the true and superior part of the human being was not the body, but the divine spirit or substance that dwelt within it. The question then became how the divine and true nature of the self could be realized, recovered, or released from the limits of the body. The answer often involved a reorientation of one's self-understanding, either through received knowledge, a form of bodily asceticism, or both. Immortality was considered an achieved state, attained by overcoming the mortal body.

The author of 2 Peter was aware of this aspiration and appeals to it in this section. Other New Testament writers appear to eschew the idea of "participating in the divine nature" probably to avoid blurring the human-divine distinction. Some use language that is semantically parallel (e.g., Rom 8:14-17; 1 Cor 3:16; 2 Cor 3:17-18), but none comes as close to the Greek metaphysical conceptions as our author does here.

◊ ◊ ◊ ◊

In this section the author employs Hellenistic concepts ("divine nature," "godliness," and "corruption") to convey his message to the audience. While he uses Greek and Roman ideas, he expresses specific reservations that distinguish his thinking from conventional thought. Thus, unlike much Greek thought, he does not regard the physical world as intrinsically corrupt, but as corrupted by human behavior. Second, he does not argue that humans can become divine, or discover their divine nature. Rather, only by God's initiative are human beings *made* participants in the divine nature.

Here, as elsewhere in the letter, the author has modified the Hellenistic concept of "divine nature" to fit the context of Christian thought. This adaptation becomes clearer when we compare this phrase to its converse, "escape from the corruption of the world." This latter phrase refers to the natural decay that characterizes the physical world and its inhabitants. As part of the created order, human beings share in its corrupted condition, but in the eschatological consummation of the world, they will be made imperishable and exempt from death. They will partake in the divine nature because they will be made incorruptible and so share in eternity (see 1:11; 3:7, 11-13). With this thought the author is in accord with other New Testament writers (e.g., 1 Cor 15:42-53), and reflects the apocalyptic underpinnings of early Christian belief.

A Response of Virtue (1:5-7)

The phrase "for this very reason" connects verses 5-7 with the preceding arguments and the author now turns to the ethical implications of the promise of "partaking in the divine nature." He presents the shape of the believer's morality by means of eight virtues, carefully constructed to present the Christian faith in the idiom of Greco-Roman culture. Six virtues stem from common Hellenistic moral instruction. Two others, rich with Christian overtones, frame them. The rhetorical construction, called a *sorites*, organizes the virtues in seven pairs by a linking technique, in which the second member of each pair is repeated as the first member of the pair that follows. This creates the appearance of a logical or necessary connection among the virtues, enabling the author to "demonstrate" how the faith that God has established among them should "naturally result" in a moral life (see Fischel, 1973, 119-151).

◊ ◊ ◊ ◊

In this section the author again uses Greco-Roman concepts to describe the Christian life. The verbs employed are a case in point. Believers are "to make every effort to support" their faith with a life of virtue. The verb *epichorēgeo* ("to support") becomes common in later Greek, but it is rare in the New Testament (2 Pet 1:5, 11; 2 Cor 9:10; Gal 3:5; Col 2:19), which makes this sentence difficult to translate. Originally the word meant to "provide a choir for a festival," which would suggest an action that enhances an already established matter. Later it came to mean, "to give lavishly, with generosity" (Kelly 1981, 306). The author probably used it to create the idea that the virtue must be added to faith in order to complete faith's effect.

Placing the virtue of "faith" at the head of the list also gives the Hellenistic moral terms a Christian cast. (For other virtue lists in the New Testament, see 2 Cor 6:6; Gal 5:22; 1 Tim 4:12, 6:11; 2 Tim 2:22, 3:10; 1 Pet 3:8; Rev 2:19. Outside the New Testament, see *1 Clem* 62:2; *Barn* 2:2.) "Faith" *(pistis)* picks up the language used in verse 1. Here, however, it refers to an act of fidelity or trust rather than the content of belief. Its use re-emphasizes that a moral life is the necessary response to the knowledge God has bestowed (v. 3).

Faith is supplemented by "virtue," a term used in Greek ethics for general moral excellence. The author used the same word in verse 3 in combination with "glory" to describe the divine character. Here the term takes its typical meaning of moral virtue and refers to a life characterized by valor and integrity. In this sense, verse 5*a* expresses a major emphasis of the letter, that moral integrity must accompany Christian faith.

Virtue is a practice, not simply an admirable quality. But in order to practice virtue, one must understand how to implement it. Accordingly, "virtue" is linked to "knowledge" *(gnōsis)*. *Gnōsis* (here distinguished from *epignōsis*) often was the first or last element in Greek ethical lists because it was considered the basis or the ultimate goal for all other virtues. Hellenistic moralists so valued knowledge because they held that good acts required proper understanding: only with right knowledge could right actions result. Here, however, faith replaces knowledge as the foundation for ethics, and *gnōsis* becomes the ability to discern faith's requirements. In effect, knowledge becomes the means by which faith's convictions are transformed into effective practices (see 2 Cor 8:7; Phil 1:9; 2 Pet 3:18).

Knowledge is coupled with "self-control" (see Acts 24:25; Gal 5:23; *1 Clem* 35:2, 62:2). "Self-control" expressed an ideal of

Stoic thought: the ability to restrain one's physical or mental desires. Here the term designates self-discipline and the avoidance of excess. Perhaps it is also included as a contrast to the self-indulgent behavior the author ascribes to the opposition in chapter 2.

"Self-control" is connected to "endurance," which in Greek philosophical instruction often pertained to "perseverance." In the New Testament it frequently denotes steadfast trust in God, especially in the face of oppression or suffering (Rom 5:31-4; 2 Cor 6:4; 1 Thess 1:3). It is possible that the author has in mind a life predicated on a trusting anticipation of the second coming (see also 3:11-13 and 14-18). If so, this expectation constitutes another contrast to the opponents, who ridicule the idea of steadfastly waiting for the Lord (3:3-4).

Endurance is paired with *eusebeia* ("godliness" or "piety"), which, as in verse 3, designates the duty one owes to God to lead a pious life. In Greek ethics it has a broader thought frame, encompassing the honor one gives to the gods, the state, and one's ancestors and family. The term may suggest still another contrast with the opposition. In 2:5-6 the cognate term "ungodly" contrasts the punishment of the impious with the rescue of the "godly" (2:9). Just as the Lord would rescue the righteous from an ungodly environment, so too will the Lord deliver the current believers if they resist the ungodly opposition.

The author next links "godliness" to "mutual affection," *(philadelphia)* the care and love expressed between family members or intimate friends (BDAG, 1055). Early Christians readily practiced such affection because they conceived of their community as a family (Rom 12:10; Gal 6:10; 1 Pet 1:22, 2:5, 2:17). The list culminates with the correlation of "mutual affection" and "love" (*agapē*). The two terms often overlapped, and they were often interchanged with no difference in meaning (LSJ, 6). In Christian discourse, however, *agapē* takes on a more specific meaning. It still refers to human love, as it does here, but God's love shown to humanity determines the shape and character of the relationships. Thus it expresses the love that extends beyond self-interest and reciprocity to actions of affection that seek the enhancement of their object. *Agapē* is frequently found in New Testament virtue lists (2 Cor 6:6; Gal 5:22; Eph 4:2; 1 Tim 6:11) and is typical of Christian exhortation (e.g., 1 Cor 8:1, 13:4, 8; 2 Cor 8:8; Gal 5:13; 1 Thess 5:8; 1 John 4:16). The author gives the term even greater weight by placing it at the conclusion of his list, making *agapē* the final, and hence, most significant of the virtues.

◊   ◊   ◊   ◊

In verses 5-7 the author urges a set of virtues that should characterize the recipients of God's promises. Because the readers are destined for eschatological redemption and to become "partners of the divine nature," they must live in a manner consistent with this future state. However, as verses 10-11 show, the converse is also true: the believer's present conduct has eschatological effects (see 3:11-15). Therefore, since God has provided the possibility and means for a "life of holiness and righteousness" (3:11), believers must take advantage of these gifts.

The author's use of the chaining technique binds the virtue list into one thought unit about the Christian moral life. Further, by placing "faith" at the beginning of the list and "love" at its end, the author implies a natural flow from faith to love. The life of virtue thus becomes both a requirement for and a result of faithful existence. Faith must manifest itself in moral action, and virtuous acts must be grounded in the faith granted to believers. The virtue list reminds the readers that their lives must reflect their status as "those who have been called by God's glory and goodness" (v. 3) to be "participants of the divine nature." But this participation is an existence yet to come. In the meantime, they must display the character of that life while living in a corrupted world.

Consequences of the Virtuous Life (1:8-11)

Because faith united with virtue forms the only appropriate response to God's promise that believers will be "partakers of the divine nature," the author now shows how this response is connected to eschatological judgment. Initially the consequences are expressed as positive (v. 8) and negative outcomes (v. 9). Then they are placed in an eschatological framework (vv. 10-11). The last two verses reiterate the call for an ethical response made in the first two verses as the author connects the initial actions of God with the addressee's expected response.

Although the phrase "therefore" connects verses 10-11 to those that immediately precede them, their language shows that verses 10-11 form the conclusion for the entire section (vv. 3-9). Thus, "your call" (v. 10) refers back to "the one who called us" (v. 3) and entering "into the eternal kingdom" (v. 11) is parallel to "participating in the divine nature" (v. 4). Finally, the admonition "to be all the more eager" (v. 10) uses a cognate of the term in verse 5 ("you must make every effort"), tying the exhortation in verse 10 to the one begun in verse 5.

◊ ◊ ◊ ◊

Verse 8 clarifies the eschatological status of those who display the virtues just listed. The believer who "truly possesses" these traits and amplifies them has truly appropriated the knowledge of Christ. The moral life grows out of the knowledge (*epignōsis*) of Christ that God has granted (see 1:3). Here the author employs another rhetorical figure, *litotes* (i.e., the affirmation of a thought by denying its opposite). The phrase reads literally "these things [the virtues just listed] do not cause you to be idle or unfruitful"; that is, virtues enable the Christian's life to be meaningful and effective, especially as witness to the truth of God's redemptive acts in Christ.

The combination of "idle" and "fruitless" is another example of the author's penchant for pairing similar terms. New Testament writers used both terms metaphorically to express that faith not displayed in actions and good character is defective. A correct understanding of God will lead to a life of integrity and moral consequence, one that "bears fruit" (Matt 3:8, 10, 21:43; Gal 5:22; Col 1:10; Jas 3:17-18). Here, as in James 2:18-26, the addressees are called to recognize that faith is demonstrated in action.

Verse 9 repeats the sense of verse 8, by way of a negative for-mulation, which heightens the degree of judgment and sanction. The absence of the virtues is not simply the lack of fruit, but a form of spiritual blindness. Once again, a synonymous pair illus-trates the author's idea, but the combination is somewhat odd. The author describes those who do not possess these virtues as "nearsighted and blind." The term "blind" often indicates a lack of spiritual understanding (Matt 15:14; 23:16-24; John 9:40-41). *Myōpazein* ("to be nearsighted"), however, occurs only here in the New Testament. The combined phrase cannot be taken liter-ally because near-sightedness is superfluous if one is blind. The pairing therefore was created for emphasis "they are blind, too shortsighted to see what is real" (so Bauckham 1983, 189; Mayor 1965, 96; cf. Kelly 1981, 300; Fornberg 1977, 53).

The author also portrays the fate of those not leading an ethi-cal life as forgetfulness and a reversion to a past existence, i.e., to "past sins." The metaphor of cleansing from sins has its roots in the Old Testament (e.g., Lev 16:30; Job 7:21) and refers to God's remission of human transgressions. The term "cleansing" is widely used in the New Testatment (Acts 15:9; Eph 5:26; Titus 2:14), often in connection to baptism (Acts 2:30, 22:16; Rom 6:3; 1 Cor 6:11; Titus 3:5). The author likely has that ritual in view here (see also Rom 3:25, Eph 2:1-2; 1 Pet 1:22; 3:21). Baptism created a break from the past life of sin and signaled the begin-ning of a life of righteousness (Rom 6:2-4, 1 Cor 6:9-11). Those who do not display moral fruit have forgotten that in baptism their past was put to death so that they could live as God's chosen holy ones (Col 3:5-17). While they have not yet returned to their former condition (2:20-22), some members of the audience prob-ably were close to reverting to previous immoral behavior. For them, this verse is as much a warning as it is an exhortation.

According to verse 10, believers are to "confirm their call and election." The term *bebaios* ("firm" or "secure"), along with its cognates, is used in the New Testament for actions that guaran-tee a contract or agreement. This word group frequently refers to a sign or symbol that ratifies an action, covenant, or promise (Mark 16:20; Rom 15:8; 1 Cor 1:6). Although it is often God or

Christ who provides the guarantee, here the believer ratifies the call through a life of virtue. Virtuous behavior is a sign of the believer's trust and reliance upon God to bring about eschatological deliverance. Those who display such trust "will never stumble," *(ou mē ptaisēte)* a cognate of the term used by Jude (see the comment on Jude 24). The term connotes a fall with severe consequences. If the believer responds to God's call with a virtuous life, this tragedy will never occur.

Verse 11 concludes the section, repeating the promise that God will deliver those he has called. The claim is now cast in terms of the eschatological reign of God, which is portrayed as a heavenly realm to be entered rather than as the overt rule of God on earth (cf. 1 Cor 6:10). The phrase, the Lord's "eternal kingdom," is another rare expression in the New Testament, but it clearly refers to a future existence (1:4 and 3:13).

◊ ◊ ◊ ◊

The climactic sentence in verses 10-11 signals again the author's two concerns: (1) moral conduct is a necessary response to God's promise of redemption, and (2) the future second coming is the final and ultimate proof of God's fidelity to the promise of redemption. Nevertheless, confirming one's call is not simply a matter of verbal confession, but definite acts of godliness, affection, and love.

Supposed Occasion of the Letter (1:12-15)

Verses 12-15 are central for an analysis of this letter. Structurally they create a transition from the compendium of Christian teaching and belief (vv. 3-11) to the author's initial responses to the charges leveled by his opponents (vv. 16-20). More importantly, the reference to the apostle Peter's imminent death (v. 14) identifies the writing as a "farewell testament," providing its readers with an essential key for understanding the letter and its occasion. By choosing the "farewell" genre and by providing the "proofs" that follow in verses 16-20, the author establishes his trustworthiness as a guide and interpreter of the fundamentals of the faith, and, simultaneously attacks the teachings offered by the opposition.

◊ ◊ ◊ ◊

"Therefore" and "these things" (v. 12) connect this section with the preceding verses. The author used the neuter plural form of "these things" in verses 8, 9, and 10. When he uses the term in verse 12, he is referring to "everything needed for life and godliness" (v. 1) and to the promised entrance into the eternal kingdom (v. 11), as well as the moral virtues which should result from these gifts. The connection between God's promises and a virtuous life confirms the addressees as the elect people of God's (v. 10), which makes it imperative that they remember the truth of the gospel and the ethics it implies. "Therefore," the author writes to ensure that these truths will always be at the forefront of the community's thought and deliberations.

To introduce the farewell testament, the author combined the future indicative form of the verb "I shall" with the adverb "always" and the present indicative of the infinitive "to remind," creating a difficult Greek construction. The general sense of the phrase, however, is that the letter will keep Peter's admonitions alive, reminding the readers of their heritage and preparing them for the days to come.

According to the author, the readers "are established in the truth that has come to you," which refers to their conversion, when the "knowledge" of God's truth was given to them (1:3-4). The author is following Jude 5 and uses a participial form to emphasize that the audience knows these things and is "established" in them. The verb "established" refers to something firmly in place, like a stone in a wall or a foundation platform (LSJ, 1644). Although the author's confident claim of the audience's stability may be somewhat hyperbolic, he is reminding them that the gospel they received provides a solid and reliable grounding for their faith. They should remember this foundation and resist every effort of the false teachers to modify it (2:1-4).

The verb "establish," along with its cognates "firmness" and "to make unsteady," are an important word set in this letter. The author uses these terms to distinguish three groups: the "stable" who remain loyal to God's call and their initial teaching (1:12); the "ignorant and unstable," who twist the scriptures to their own destruction (3:16); and the "unstable or unsteady souls," who are on the verge of abandoning their beliefs (2:14). For the present, the audience belongs to the first group, but, influenced by the opposition's teaching, they could easily become members of the second or third groups (3:17). The author writes to prevent this (2:20-21) and to exhort them to remain loyal "lest [they] be carried away with the error of lawless ones and lose [their] own stability" (3:17).

The last phrase in verse 12, "the truth that has come to you," is functionally equivalent to the expression in Jude 3, "the faith once and for all delivered to the saints," and refers to the initial teaching the audience received. The gospel message was often called "the truth" among early Christians (Col 1:5-6; Gal 5:7; Eph 1:13) and the author uses a similar phrase at 2:2 when he calls the Christian life "the way of truth." This phrase begins his counter-argument against those who claim that new teaching is required to ensure growth in the faith. According to the author, the church needs no new formulations of the truth, because it already possesses everything necessary to please God (1:3-11). At best, any new teaching only repeats what they already possess and at worst, it twists the gospel into a message that will lead them astray (2:2-3; 3:17).

Verse 13 signals the importance of remembering the foundational teaching. For a second time the author reminds his readers of the initial message they received from the apostles. The NRSV translation "refresh your memory" obscures the fact that the verb "to remind" was just used in verse 12. There, eschatological hope motivated the reminder (1:10-11). Here, the thought is extended, and "Peter" declares that it is his duty as an apostle to remind them of the truth (see also Moses' farewell address in Josephus, *Ant.* 4, 177-193). The author argues that "Peter's" teaching about the future coming is not optional, nor are the exhortations and warnings that follow. They are necessary charges to the congregation. The letter is not simply a final address, but an essential authoritative instance of Peter's apostolic teaching.

Peter refers to his death as the "putting off of my tent." The comparison of the human body to a tent was commonplace (see *Wis* 9:15; 2 Cor 5:1, 4). The metaphor evokes images of movement, impermanence, and pilgrimage. A tent is not a final dwelling place, but a temporary abode, and the human body should not be considered the final form of human existence. Life on earth is transitory, but eventually the faithful will dwell (1:11) in a permanent place.

In verse 14, the author combines the tent imagery with another metaphor for transition: the removal of an outer garment. Both figures suggest that the temporary body be laid aside so that at the moment of death, the spirit is released. Thus, like a tent, or a coat, the temporary form of cover is distinguished from that which it protects. The essential nature of the human being is thus the enduring spirit and not the temporary body, hence one should attend to thoughts and actions that enhance the spirit rather than indulge in bodily pleasure.

Verse 14 also supplies the supposed reason "Peter" is writing; he is to die soon, so he must ensure that his charges are prepared for his departure. When Peter says that he knows that his death will come "quickly" *(tachinos)*, he means either that it will occur in the near future or that it will occur suddenly. The context suggests that *tachinōs* is a reference to the time rather than the mode of Peter's death.

Peter knows that his death will come soon because Christ has revealed this insight to him. There are two facets of this revelation that require comment: the use of the verb "has made clear to me" (NRSV) and the possible biblical references to Christ's prediction of Peter's death. The revelation of the hero's imminent death was typically included in "farewell" testaments so its appearance here is to be expected (cf. John 13:36; Acts 9:16, 21:11). Immediately after this section, the author refers to another of these revelations (1:16-20). In both cases, God or

Christ directly informs Peter, lending weight to the remarks and establishing his authority to speak.

What incident did the author have in mind when he referred to Christ's revelation of Peter's death? Scholars have offered various possibilities ranging from Jesus' statement in John 21:18 to Peter's encounter with the risen Christ outside of Rome recorded in a second- or third-century tradition (*Acts Pet.* 35). Probably these later Christian materials, including 2 Peter and the Gospel of John (see also *1 Clem* 5:1-4), reflect an earlier tradition about Peter's death suggesting that the author had no specific text in mind when he wrote. As Kelly notes, "[i]t came naturally to Christians to believe that the heroes of the faith received premonitions of their death approaching martyrdom (e.g., Acts 20:25 and 21:11 of Paul; *Mart. Pol.* 5.2; *Pass. Perp. Fel.* 4:3-10; *Vita Cypr.* 12). The same motive was probably at work here, and it is fruitless to hunt around for any particular incident, historical or legendary" (Kelly 1981, 314).

In verse 15 "Peter" reminds the church for the third time of their initial teaching. In verses 12 and 13 he spoke of the need to remind them while he was alive; in verse 15 the reference is to the time after his death, implying that his concerns about the congregation extend beyond the present time frame. So he "will make every effort" to ensure that the church can "recall these things" after his departure. The author again uses the same verb as in 1:5 and 1:10, which expresses "Peter's" earnest desire to provide for their needs. Despite the use of the future tense, the author is referring to the letter he is currently writing (see *2 Apoc. Bar.* 78:5, cited by Bauckham 1983, 201). "Peter" will include in this letter everything necessary for the readers' future reflections. If they accept it, then they will have all they need to remain faithful.

The last phrase of verse 15 includes another metaphor for death—departure *(exodos)*. The reference is natural for those who believe in another existence beyond this life. One leaves physical existence to enter into a new state. "Life" goes on in another sphere, and death is not termination but the moment of departure or transition. The metaphor is apt, and its use contrasts with the author's reference to the "entry into heaven" (v. 11). At death one leaves *(exodos)* this world and, having remained true to the gospel, enters into *(eisodos)* the eternal kingdom of Jesus Christ.

◊　◊　◊　◊

Verse 15 serves as a concluding statement about the letter's purpose, and verses 12-15 provide the reasons "Peter" has written. He has sent a "final testament" because "false teachers" will arise (2:1) and the church will need to remember its initiatory teachings (1:19). Because he has warned and forearmed them for the future crisis, the audience will be able to persevere and withstand falsehood.

Casting the letter as a "farewell testament" allowed the author to address the challenges and objections raised by his opposition. He establishes the letter's instructions as a consistent part of the original apostolic teaching. Further, by presenting his position as Peter's *last* testament the author demonstrates that these are not random thoughts or incidental ideas, but the final and considered words of the apostle, delivered to address the needs of the congregation for years to come (1:15). As a consequence, they must be followed closely. Finally, because the "last testament" often spoke directly of future opposition and crises, it provided the author with a means for portraying his opponents as villains, whom the apostle predicted would come to lead believers astray (2:1-3).

By including the term "always," the author maintains that the testament applied not only to the short periods before and after Peter's death, but to all future threats and situations as well. In fact, as 2:1-2 and 3:1-4 show, Peter left the testament precisely for moments such as the present one, when "false teachers" and "scoffers" would threaten the community's faith and existence. The fiction of the "last testament" form provides the author a means to counter false teaching because it "predicts" the opposition's presence while simultaneously recalling the true teaching that the apostle Peter wanted them to hold.

The First Apologetic Response (1:16-21)

Although he does not address the opposition's teaching specifically until 3:16-21, the author offers an indirect response in

1:16. He is countering a charge that the proclamation of the second coming was no longer a tenet of the gospel message. In a two-part reply, he argues that (1) the teaching about the second coming is based on an actual event and therefore cannot be a myth (1:16-18); and (2) that inspired interpretation of Old Testament prophecy ratifies the teaching, so it is not mere human opinion (1:19-21). The initial "historical" evidence for the reality of the future second coming is provided by the transfiguration of Jesus. Scripture is then invoked to prove that a future judgment is part of God's plan.

Reply to Objections: Eyewitness Proof (1:16-18)

Verse 16 uses a common syntactic contrast, "not x but y," found six times in this letter: three of these (1:16; 1:21, 3:9a), display elements of the opposition's teaching. Neyrey, citing other ancient instances of the structure (especially from Philo), has suggested that 2 Peter employs this construction because it was a standard rhetorical device of refutation (see Neyrey 1980, 507-508). Whether or not the antithesis structure was a technical device for refutation, it is likely that verse 16a reflects the opposition's charges and that verses 16b-18 provide the author's response.

◊ ◊ ◊ ◊

According to the false teachers, anyone who taught that the second coming would occur follows "cleverly devised myths." Greek writers used the word *mythos* in many different ways, ranging from references to ancient explanatory legends to stories that predicted future realities. Frequently myths were distinguished from genuine arguments because they were not based on tangible evidence or actual accounts. If "myths" were considered true it was only in a limited sense, i.e., as stories or fables to illustrate a point that could be established on rational and objective grounds. The value of myths was in their hortatory possibilities, not as proof or historical account. Diodorus of Sicily expresses it well: "For it is true that the myths *(mythologia)* which are related about Hades, in spite of the fact that their subject matter is fictitious *(peplasmenēn hypothesin),* contribute greatly to fostering piety *(eusebeian)* and justice *(dikaiosynēn)* among men" *(Hist.* 1.2.2) (quoted by Neyrey 1993, 175). Ancient Greek moralists associated myths in this sense with fabrication and so criticized them as stories that were used to control the naïve or unsuspecting (Neyrey 1993, 175). Thus, when the opposition charged that accounts of the second coming were myths, they were dismissing them as untrue or, at best, only useful for moral exhortation or control of the spiritually immature. In either case, those who taught the doctrine were charged with lying or duping their audiences.

Later in the epistle the author will reverse these charges and insinuate that it is the opposition who cause people to follow immoral paths and corrupt the truth (2:2). At this point, however, the author simply responds to the opponents' charge that the author's teaching was based on fantastic myths.

The adjective "cleverly devised" amplifies this negative conception of the apostolic teaching about the second coming, characterizing it as a story created for the purpose of deception. This suggests that the opposition considered the teaching about future judgment not simply a myth, but a human fabrication devised for duping. The position is similar to Greek philosophical criticisms of those who believed that the gods had influence on human behavior (e.g., Epicureans and other rationalist philosophers). The position also mirrors critics who maintained that narratives about reward and punishment were ill-founded myths used for coercive controls of popular morality (Bauckham 1983, 214; Neyrey 1993, 175).

The author's opponents held a similar view. They were arguing that the teaching of future judgment was no more than a story devised to create fear among new Christians to motivate their moral obedience. This teaching should be disregarded once a Christian was more mature, for it was incompatible with the story of God's gracious acceptance and redemption of the believer through Christ. God might act in the world to come, but it would not be for the purpose of judgment.

In response, the author argues that the teaching about the second coming is based on eyewitness reports and so could not be a myth, but was in fact the result of a cogent reflection on the evidence God had provided. Since prophetic scripture also records the teaching, it could not be a new belief, but must be one God has already established.

The author now shifts from the first person singular "I" of verses 12-15 to the first person plural "we" (vv. 16-18). This underscores that Peter was accompanied by other select apostles granted special access to the revelation of Christ's glory. New Testament references to divine revelation often contain the verb "make known" (e.g., Luke 2:15; John 15:15; Rom 16:26; Eph 1:9, 3:3, 5, 10, 6:19; Col 1:27). Here it indicates that the apostles were conveying God's truth when they preached Christ's future appearance.

The NRSV phrase "power and coming" could suggest that the author meant that the apostolic teaching focused both on Christ's power and second coming, but that was likely not his meaning. While the author acknowledges Christ's power as the source of life and godliness (1:3), here he again is combining two terms, "power" and "coming," in order to highlight the public nature of the *Parousia*. A better translation of the phrase would be "powerful coming" or "coming in power" because this enables modern readers to recognize that the main controversy was not over the possibility of the future appearance, but its nature, particularly Christ's role as ultimate judge (so also Fornberg 1977, 79-80).

Parousia means "presence" and was used to connote the appearance of a deity or a significant person (such as the emperor or a conquering general). Some scholars have suggested that the term refers to Christ's *first* appearance on earth. The internal and external evidence, however, argues against this interpretation. First, the author uses the term two other times (3:4, 12), and in both instances he means the exalted Christ's *second* coming. Second, the entire epistle is geared toward the refutation of faulty teaching about the future, not disputes about Christ's earthly existence. Third, in the New Testament, the word is almost a technical term for Christ's appearance at the Eschaton (e.g., Matt 24:3; 1 Cor 15:23; 1 Thess 2:19, 4:15; Jas 5:7; and is used as a synonym for Jesus' second coming in New Testament scholarship). Finally, although *Parousia* was used to refer to Christ's first appearance on earth, this was not regularly the case until the second and third centuries by Justin, Origen, and Eusebius (see Fornberg 1977, 80). Thus, it is likely that the author intended *Parousia* to be understood as a reference to the second coming here and throughout the letter.

The author refers to himself and the others as "eyewitnesses" of Christ's "majesty," the moment when James, John, and Peter saw Jesus transfigured into his full glory (cf. Matt 17:2; Mark 9:2-3; Luke 9:29-31). The word "eyewitness" is a *hapax legomenon* in the New Testament (a verbal cognate is used in 1 Pet 2:12 and 3:2). Elsewhere in Greek literature the term refers to an observer or spectator (as in 1 Pet 2:12). It also designated initiates of the mystery religions: i.e., those who had seen the sacred cult rituals or experienced a vision (see Fornberg 1977, 123). Most likely the author intended the standard use of the term (i.e., observer), but his tendency to use Hellenistic religious terminology suggests that he was aware of the other connotation, so the use of "eyewitness" also could imply that the apostles had a unique and privileged status as divine initiates.

The use of the term "majestic" interprets what the apostles saw: the divine nature of the Christ. This term was commonly used to describe God's glory and splendor (LXX Dan 7:27; Josephus *Ant.* §§1.24; 8.111); here, however, it has been applied to Christ. In the transfiguration, the "majesty" of God was bestowed on Jesus, commissioning him as God's divine agent (cf. Luke 9:28-35). Christ's status is implicit in verse 16, but the repetition of "majesty" shows it was the author's intent to make this explicit in verse 17.

Verses 17 and 18 describe the revelation in more detail, shifting from the visual imagery in verse 16 to a description of an auditory experience. The voice from heaven pronouncing Jesus as God's "beloved son" and the mountain locale indicate that the author is referring to the event known as the transfiguration.

There are however, significant differences between 2 Peter and the Synoptic accounts. Second Peter contains no mention of specific apostles (other than Peter), or the appearance of Moses and Elijah, or the building of shelters. The shining nature of Christ's appearance, the cloud, the subsequent behavior of the disciples, and the command to listen to the beloved Son are also absent (for a full list of differences, see Bauckham 1983, 205-210).

These differences suggest that the author was not dependent on the Synoptics for his material, but had access to another transfiguration account (so also Bauckham 1983, 206-207). They also show that both the author and the Synoptic writers adapted the Transfiguration tradition for their own purposes. Thus, while the Synoptic gospels present the transfiguration as a sanction of Jesus as the Christ or as a divine sanction of his coming death (Matt 16:24-28, 17:5; Mark 8:31, 9:6; Luke 9:21-27, 35 respectively), our author uses it to establish Christ's role as coming judge.

Both the Synoptic writers and our author considered the transfiguration as a commissioning of Christ by God. The bestowal of "glory and honor," as well as the exclamation that Christ is God's "beloved son," indicates that Jesus has been designated as God's special agent. The phrase "honor and glory" is another of 2 Peter's typical word pairs, but it is also a stock phrase often used to denote honorable qualities (e.g., Ps 8:5 [cited in Heb 2:7, 9]; Rom 2:7, 10; 1 Pet 1:7). The author uses it to show that the transfiguration was a clear manifestation of Jesus' divine commission and authority. In distinction from the Synoptics, where the commission ratifies that Jesus will carry out God's redemptive mission on earth, the author of 2 Peter presents the event as Christ's installation as eschatological ruler and future judge of creation (so too Bauckham 1983, 205).

The Synoptics compare Jesus' appearance to an intense white brightness (Matt 17:2; Mark 9:2-3; Luke 9:29), which indicates the presence of God's splendor and is a sign of Jesus' future exalted status. 2 Peter makes the same connection, as the circumlocution for God, "the Majestic Glory," demonstrates (see *1 Enoch* 14:20; *Test Lev* 3:4; Ps 145:5, 19). God, the possessor and essence of glory, bestows glory on his Son, thus designating him as God's anointed one. The disciples *see* Jesus receiving "glory and honor" from God, and they also *hear* the heavenly voice proclaim his status. The phrase reads literally "a voice was borne to him by the Majestic Glory," emphasizing that God communicates this authority. The disciples hear the voice proclaim, "This is my Son, my Beloved, with whom I am well pleased." In actuality, it is better to say that they *overhear* this, for the words are not spoken to the disciples, but are "conveyed to him" (i.e., Jesus). This is a divine decree, akin to the designation of the King by Yahweh reported in Ps 2:7, and the apostles merely observe it. The transaction is between God and Christ, not between God and the witnesses.

The text repeats the possessive pronoun "my" ("this is *my* Son, *my* beloved"), which emphasizes Jesus' status as *God's* chosen one. The use of the emphatic pronoun "I" in the phrase "with whom I am well pleased" further stresses his status. Throughout, the focus has been on God's designation of Jesus as his eschatological agent. Jesus receives God's glory and honor, the heavenly voice addresses him, and God himself chooses him to reign.

The apostles heard the voice "come from heaven" while they were with Jesus "on the holy mountain." In Jewish tradition the *bat kol* ("the voice from heaven communicating the echo of God's voice") announced God's will and judgment (e.g., Dan 4:31; *1 Enoch* 65:4). The early Christians used this idea to announce God's revelation (Mark 1:11; John 12:8; Rev 10:4, 8). The disembodied voice and the use of the circumlocution "Majestic Glory" communicate the transcendent nature of God. The apostles' role as private witnesses to this event underscores the veracity and singularity of their teaching about the commission of Christ as future judge.

The phrase "on the holy mountain" likely reflects Ps 2:6, where Zion is referred to as "the holy hill." According to the psalm, on this hill God appoints the king. The apostles were with Jesus on the holy hill when God designated him eschatological judge. In witnessing Christ's bestowed glory they saw that God had anointed Christ as the king who will reign over all the earth (see Ps 2:8-9).

◊ ◊ ◊ ◊

In this relatively short section the author presents an impressive array of evidence to demonstrate the truth of the teaching about the second coming. First, in the transfiguration God designated Jesus as the eschatological judge to come. Second, the apostles were present "with him." As a result they both saw and heard God's bestowal of glory upon Jesus. Thus, on the grounds of eyewitness evidence and God's own declaration, the author establishes the second coming as an essential and original part of the gospel message. Since it is an objective event, separate from the tellers themselves, it is not a clever myth, but a genuine report of God's own actions and purposes. When the apostles speak of the second coming, they are reporting an important aspect of the true nature of Jesus' transfiguration by God, not some fabrication.

The author's account emphasizes the story's commissioning features, especially those which draw on Psalm 2:6-7: the setting on a "holy hill" and the proclamation "you are my son" designating Jesus as God's divine agent. Early Christians applied this messianic tradition to Jesus and understood this psalm as a prophecy of his anointing by God (Matt 3:17; Acts 13:33; Heb 1:5, 5:5; Rev 2:26).

Our author does not present the transfiguration as a revelation of Jesus' hidden identity, but as the occasion when he received "honor and glory" from God, i.e., when he was installed by God as eschatological Lord (so Bauckham 1983, 212; Kelly 1981, 318; Neyrey 1993, 173). Second Peter is not the only instance where the fact of the transfiguration is connected with the fact of the second coming. Both ancient and modern interpreters have made the link between the transfiguration and Jesus' future coming, e.g., *Apocalypse of Peter* (see Neyrey 1993, 173-174 and Kee 1972, 149).

Further Reply to Objections: Prophetic Proof (1:19-21)

The chapter's final verses provide a second response to the opposition's objections. As in verses 16-18, the author presents warrants for believing in Christ's return. Whereas those verses provided eyewitness evidence, here the argument is based on authoritative prophecy.

Early Christians often used Old Testament texts to shape, understand, and express and support their beliefs. Apparently the opponents questioned the use of the Old Testament for proving the validity of "orthodox" interpretation of the second coming. The opposition would have agreed that the Scripture contained prophecy about the Messiah, but they would have rejected any interpretation of the prophecy that inferred Christ's second coming as eschatological judge. The author writes in order to show that interpreting prophecy as referring to the second coming is not only correct, but divinely inspired.

Formally, the opponents' charge is implied in verse 20 and the author's rebuttal argument follows in verse 21. The pattern of argument thus mirrors that found in verses 16-18 as the repetition of the "not . . . but" phrasing shows. Debates about the nature of prophecy occurred frequently among both Jews and Christians and the author's arguments in verse 21 draw freely on this stock material (e.g., his use of "own," "moved by the Holy Spirit," and "from God").

Because of its grammatical and linguistic features, verse 19 is a *crux interpretum* (so also Neyrey 1993, 178). Three issues are particularly difficult to settle: (1) the identity of "the prophetic message," (2) whether to interpret "confirmed" as a comparative or superlative adjective, and (3) the meaning of the phrase "until the day dawns and the morning star rises in your hearts."

Although commentators have proposed numerous understandings of the phrase "prophetic message" *(prophētikon logon)* it was used most often as a reference to Scripture, whether in part or in whole (so also Bauckham 1983, 224). It is likely that here the phrase refers either to the entire Old Testament as Scripture or to specific portions from the Old Testament that were applied to the second coming. If our author had in mind particular texts,

Num 24:17, Ps 2:9, and Dan 7:13-14 would be possible candidates.

He was using the phrase to argue that belief in the second coming was not a recent idea, but was based on scriptural prophecy. Our author also argued that this prophecy is itself "more fully confirmed" (*bebaioteron*). *Bebaioteron* is the comparative form of the adjective *bebaios*, which means "firm" or "permanent" (BDAG, 172-173). The NRSV translation, "we have the prophetic message more fully confirmed" allows for the comparative force of the adjective, but it leaves the comparison unclear, causing one to ask, "More fully confirmed than what?"

As a result of the anomalies created by translating *bebaioteron* as a comparative, the majority of commentators attribute it superlative force and translate it as "very firm." This yields a paraphrase something like "and we have the very firm prophetic message," or "we possess the prophetic word as something that is (now) all the more reliable" (BDAG, 172; see also Bauckham 1983, 223 and Neyrey 1980, 515). The author is arguing that belief in the second coming rests on two solid pieces of evidence: the eyewitness experience of the transfiguration and a reliable prophetic word. In verses 20-21 he will explain why prophetic scripture and its interpretation can be considered trustworthy.

Accepting the validity of the prophetic message, the author enjoins his readers to let it guide their daily lives. The phrase "you will do well" has the force of an imperative (Fornberg 1977, 84). The readers must heed the Scripture "as a lamp shining in a dark place." The image of the word of the Lord as a lamp occurs often in the Old Testament (Ps 119:105, Job 29:3, Prov 6:23, *Wis* 18:4) as well as in later writings (*2 Bar* 17:4; 59:2; 77:13-16). As a contrast to the lamp's light, the author of 2 Peter has used a very unusual word, "dark place" to indicate where this lamp burns. The word appears nowhere else in the New Testament, but it is found in Aristotle's *De Color* 3, as an antonym of *lampros* ("bright") (BDAG, 154). The probable sense is that the prophetic word stands out from the darkness of the world, illuminating the minds and paths of believers. They can and must rely upon it to avoid stumbling (1:10) while they wait for the coming day of God (3:12).

The author has also chosen an unusual phrase to refer to the last day, and the phrase "in your hearts" also causes some confusion for modern readers. Other passages in 2 Peter show that the author understood the second coming as an objective, public event, not a private one (see e.g., 3:3-13). Thus, it is surprising to find a phrase that suggests it is a matter of internal experience. Some commentators solve this problem by arguing that the author is not actually referring to the second coming, but to a moment of full internal enlightenment that occurs before the second coming (Mayor 1965, 111). This is doubtful, since other New Testament writers use this same imagery (the dawning day and the appearance of the morning star) to refer to Christ's return. Others admit that the author is referring to the audience members' inner selves, but distinguish this internal realization from the external appearance (Kelly 1981, 323). Bauckham (1983, 226) and Fornberg (1977, 85) offer a variation on this reading, which minimizes its implications of privatized experiences. They argue that the phrase refers only to one aspect of the second coming: the fact that prophecy becomes unnecessary when full revelation has occurred. In this case "in your hearts" is equivalent to full understanding and knowledge created by the external reality (cf. 1 Cor 13:8-12 and Jer 31:31-34).

The same sentiment is presented in verse 19. The second coming is not a private or individual event, but the public appearance of Christ as the cosmic Lord. Still, only when that full revelation does occur, will all individuals know who and what Christ is. Thus, the day will "dawn in their hearts," and knowledge will make prophecy and instruction unnecessary. While the author does acknowledge a subjective experience, he is not trying to give a "psychological orientation" to the second coming (cf. Kelly 1981, 323). Neither is he substituting a subjective event for an objective one, since this would defeat his argument for the reality of a future judgment. Rather, he expected an imminent second coming during the lifetime of his audience (1:19, 3:14) that would fully reveal the reality of Christ.

In verse 19 the author uses two standard images for Christ's return. One of these, "the dawning day" was used by early Christians to refer to the end of the eschatological age (Matt 10:15, 12:36; Acts 2:2; 1 Pet 2:12) as well as to the second coming itself (Rom 13:12; 1 Cor 1:8; Phil 1:6, 10; 1 Thess 5:2; 2 Thess 2:2). The dawning day stands in contrast to the darkness of the present time and hints at the more technical phrase, "the day of the Lord," when the Lord will be acknowledged as sovereign of the cosmos and will execute judgment on the unrighteous. Then, the second coming will fulfill the promise of salvation and initiate the moment of punishment for the unrighteous (2: 9 and see the comment on Jude 6).

The second image, "the morning star" *(phōsphoros),* literally means "light bearer." The ancients used it to refer to the planet Venus, which often appears at dawn in the northern sky. The term may also be an allusion to Num 24:17 (LXX) "a star shall come out of Jacob," a text some Second Temple Jews already interpreted as a messianic prophecy (1QM 11:6-7; *CD* 7:18-20; *T. Levi* 18:3). Its echo here connects the appearance of the Messiah with the final day (Rev 2:28, 22:16).

The introductory phrase in verse 20, "First of all you need to understand this," signals that this prophetic evidence is a of crucial importance to the author and his audience (see also 3:3). Before any consideration of the second coming can occur, the nature of the scriptural interpretation must be understood. The author thus moves to his main point: "no prophecy of scripture is a matter of one's own interpretation." The phrasing is ambiguous: it can mean either that the listener is interpreting or that the speaker who delivers the statement or symbolic saying is doing so.

Typically, one would connect "one's own" with the hearer of prophecy, but the term was also used to deny the human origin of prophecy (especially by Philo, e.g., *Mos*.1.281, 286; Bauckham 1983, 229-230). Taken this way, the phrase implies that any prophecy is actually a two-fold action of God: an initial inspiration providing a prophet with an utterance or vision and a second inspiration that provides an interpretation of the statement, symbolic act, or vision. Amos, for example, announces his vision of a summer basket and then presents the Lord's interpretation of the symbol (Amos 8:1-3). Thus, the interpretation is not "the prophet's own," but from the Lord.

Nevertheless, this translation of "one's own" as "the prophet's own interpretation" is quite awkward and most modern commentators take "one's own" as a reference to the individual hearer (see Kelly 1981, 323-324). This yields the sense that legitimate interpretation of prophecy is not a matter of individual whim, but an objective statement outside the control of the individual, since it comes from God. Since it is from inspiration and not from human design, the interpretation bears divine authority. As a result, prophetic witness is the basis for human understanding, and therefore on par with the transfiguration as verification for the truth of the apostolic teaching about the second coming.

The term "interpretation" occurs only here in the New Testament. The cognate verb form appears in Mark 4:34 and in Acts 19:39, where it refers to explanations of an enigmatic statement or the solution of a difficulty. Here the noun refers to an explanation or interpretation of the "prophetic word." The writer admits that there is something to be interpreted, but denies that the interpretation is grounds for a debate because "no prophecy ever came by human will, but by men and women moved by the Holy Spirit."

The double use of *pherein* ("came by" and "moved by") underscores the contrast between human and divine. Prophecy is the result not of human desire or invention, but of divine initiative. Implicitly then, the true interpretation of prophecy does not *come* from humans but to those *moved* by the Spirit. As such, both the prophetic utterance and its interpretation are inspired and reflect the "word of God." *Pherein* is also used at 1:17-18 where the writer referred to God's designation of Jesus as the "beloved son." Just as the heavenly voice conveyed the proper interpretation of the transfigured Jesus, so God provides the true interpretation of prophetic utterance.

◊ ◊ ◊ ◊

In verses 20-21 the author is responding to a charge that the "apostolic" teaching about future judgment was not consistent with the prophetic scripture; it was only human opinion and did not reflect a genuine understanding of scripture. In response, the author argues that no genuine interpretation of scripture is a matter of human will. Thus, his own interpretation (or that of the apostles) was not a matter of choice but obedience, and the apostles were simply handing on what the Holy Spirit had inspired.

The author's terms, particularly the combination of "moved by" with "the spirit" in verse 21, echo language found in Greek religion, where prophetic activity is called "being borne by a god" *(theophoros)* (see Philo, *Spec. Leg.* 1: 65 and Justin, *1 Apol.* 36, 37 for similar language). The author's arguments however, are based on the Old Testament concept that the genuine prophet only speaks at the urging of God (Jer 1:4-10, 14:14, 23:16; Ezek 13:1-7). The consistent appearance of the issue shows how frequently Jewish and Hellenistic circles (including Christianity) questioned the legitimacy of prophetic activity.

Probably the author had appealed to a prophecy as evidence for the second coming, but the opposition rejected this interpretation of the prophetic words. As a result, he argues that prophecy *and* its interpretation originate with God so it is a valid guide to the Christian's existence (v. 19). Moreover, since God's Spirit grants the interpreter understanding of God's word, when the opposition rejects the interpretation of the prophetic word, it is debating not with the author but with God's own Spirit. This action identifies them as enemies of God, who "deny their Master" (2:1). In the next chapter, the author exposes them as false teachers and shows how they create dissension and destruction in the community of faith.

False Teachers and Final Judgment (2:1-3*a*)

The goal of the present section and those that follow (2:3*b*-10*a*, 10*b*-16, and 16-22) is to expose the opposition as false teachers (2:1) who propound destructive opinions and sow dissension. Since he holds that the past can serve as a guide to the present, the author draws an analogy between ancient Israel and the present believers. Just as Israel ("the people" v. 1) knew both genuine and false prophets, so God's current people should expect to find impostors alongside genuine representatives.

Here the author has made extensive use of Jude as a source and guide (see Introduction). In 2:1-3*a* the author borrows from Jude 4 the terms "immorality," "master," and "denying," as well as the charges of surreptitious behavior (v. 1) and foreordained judgment (v. 3). These three verses introduce a shift from the general exhortations and warnings of chapter 1 to a sustained polemic against the false teachers (2:1-22). From the beginning of the letter, the author has had his opponents and their teaching in mind, and hints of this concern surfaced in the letter's first chapter. For example, the author insisted on the moral component of faith (1:5-7), probably because he believed that the opposing teachers encouraged moral laxity. Likewise the references to the reality of eschatological events (1:11 and 1:16) anticipate his charge that the opponents deny the truth of the second coming (3:4-7). With 2:1-3*a*, the implicit criticism turns into explicit charges.

◊ ◊ ◊ ◊

The author identifies the opposition as "false teachers" whose real desires and motives are hidden from the congregation. Unlike Jude 4, the charge is not that the teachers steal into the community, but rather that their teaching is "smuggled in." The rare verb "bring in" can mean "to introduce" in a neutral sense, but it can also suggest underhanded or surreptitious activity, the likely meaning here (see also Gal 2:4). The furtive manner of entry implies malicious purpose. While they pose as helpers, the teachers are bent on exploiting the church.

These teachers bring "destructive opinions" *(haireseis apōleian)* into the church. The noun *hairesis* eventually came to have the meaning "heresy," but initially it designated a school of thought or a different opinion (see 1 Cor 11:18 and Gal 5:20). The derogatory sense is intended here, but exactly how or why the other teaching would lead to destruction is not yet evident. The term *apōleian*, which the author always uses with respect to the final judgment, signals that their end is eschatological ruin. The word appears three times in this section and is repeated throughout the letter (2:1, 3; 3:7; 16; see also the cognate *apollynai*, 3:6, 9). Its repetition here, coupled with the use of "perish" in 3:6, 9, shows that the author considered incorrect comprehension of final judgment a fatal error.

The author describes the opponents as "those who deny their Master." Again, the source is Jude 4, as the use of *despotēs* ("Master") and *arnoumenoi* ("deniers") show (see comment on Jude 4). While Jude judged his opponents' denial of the Master to be a form of disobedience to God's revealed will, our author considered it a rejection of Christ's role as cosmic judge (1:9-11, 16; 2:9-10; 3:4-7, 8-10).

The expression "the one who bought them" refers to Christ's ransom of humanity by his death (see 1 Cor 6:20, 7:23; Gal 3:13). The metaphor was drawn from the Greco-Roman practice of buying and selling slaves. Once a slave's freedom was purchased, he or she owed complete allegiance to the purchaser. Since Christ purchased the freedom of believers who were enslaved to sin (see 1:4, 2:21), all believers should seek to serve Christ with full obedience to his will. Instead, as its teaching reveals, the opposition has violated the terms of manumission. Hence they will be punished with "swift destruction."

They will be condemned, not because God has revoked their redemption, but as the result of their behavior. The false teachers "bring in" *(pareisagō)* new and erroneous teachings, and this action "brings upon them" *(epagō)* their future destruction. This destiny is a tragic irony: it is the teachers rejection of future judgment that condemns them when that judgment does occur.

Their destruction will be "swift" *(tachinēn,* as in 1:14). This term is an oblique criticism of the false teachers' own belief (3:4, 9). The teachers mock those who believe in the imminent return of Christ and ask, "Where is the promise of his coming?" In chapter three the author will refute those taunts. Here he simply predicts their swift destruction as evidence against their teaching.

Their own destruction is terrible enough, but even more damning is their responsibility for the ruin of other believers. The "many" who will follow are members of the church who align themselves with the teachers. The verb *exakolouthēsousin* ("to follow"), which appears in no other New Testament writing, is used three times in 2 Peter (1:16, 2:1, 15), always in the context of doctrine or teaching. In 1:16 the author declared that he did not follow cleverly devised myths, but was an eyewitness of truth. Its repetition here contrasts his steadfastness with the instability of those who abandon the truth to follow the false teachers.

The author describes the alternative teaching that the "many" have now adopted as "licentious ways" *(aselgeiais)*. The term typically refers to immoral behavior (see also 2:7, 18), often sexual in nature (BDAG, 141). Those who now follow the false teachers have not simply altered some incidental beliefs; they have exchanged virtue for debauchery.

Whether the new followers (or the teachers themselves) actually engaged in immoral behavior is unclear. Some commentators suggest that the teachers did promote immoral behavior because they taught their followers that they were free from future judgment (Bauckham 1983, 241). There are reasons, however, to conclude that the author's charges of immoral behavior are a rhetorical convention. First, charging opponents with immoral behavior and claiming that following their teaching would result in an irresolute life was a stock element of ancient polemic (Neyrey 1993, 191). Second, in ancient philosophical schools, the idea that corrupt thought would inevitably result in corrupt behavior was commonplace. Jesus makes a similar connection with his statement about defilement: "But what comes out of the mouth proceeds from the heart, and this is what defiles. For out of the heart come evil intentions, murder, adultery, fornication, theft, false witness, slander." (Matt 15:18-19). The author uses the same logic to argue that the teachers' beliefs inevitably lead to immoral behavior. Third, since the author is following Jude 4, even using the same term for immorality, the accusation may be more a convention of rhetoric than criticism of actual immoral behavior.

The author indicts the teachers not only for the effect the new teaching had on the life of the congregation, but also for the damage they caused to the church's reputation. The NRSV translation of *di' hous* ("because of these teachers") is misleading. More likely the author was referring to the immoral behavior of their adherents, i.e., "because of the followers' inappropriate behavior" non-Christian neighbors questioned the validity of Christian beliefs. The teachers instigated the bad behavior, but the congregants scandalized the larger society of non-believers.

The phrase "way of truth" refers to the totality of the Christian life, its teaching and requisite mode of conduct. The author uses the term *hodos* ("way") three other times in this chapter: 2:15 (twice), and 2:21. Here and at verse 21 "the way of righteousness" denotes the Christian life, while in verse 15 the rejection of that life is in view. The expression "the way" was commonly used in the Old Testament for human conduct and eventually became a technical term in Jewish ethical writing concerning "the two ways"—the way of righteousness and the way of injustice or wickedness. Early Christians adopted the term as a shorthand expression for their movement and its life (see particularly Acts 9:2; 19:9, 23; 24:14, 22, "the way"; Acts 18:25, "the way of the Lord"; Acts 18:26, "the way of God"). Verse 15, where the "straight road" is contrasted with the "way of Balaam," reflects the Jewish ethical contrast.

This section concludes in verse 3*a* with a double charge against the teachers. First, they are greedy and interested in the congregation only as a means for monetary gain. The term *emporeuesthai* ("to exploit") could mean simply "to carry on business," but most likely the idea of cheating or "trafficking in something" is intended, so that the author is charging the teachers with turning the gospel message into a commodity to be marketed for profit; cf. 2:15-16.

Second, the teachers speak with "deceptive words" *(plastois logois)*. The adjective *plastois* suggests that they change their teaching in form or content to ensure their own benefit. Their words were mere tools of convenience, to be manipulated whenever circumstances allow (see the comment on Jude 11). In 1:16

the author denied following "cleverly devised myths" and provided proof that his teaching was faithful to the gospel. Now he charges the other teachers with fabricating their message for the purpose of monetary gain.

◊ ◊ ◊ ◊

We noted in the comments on 1:12-15 that farewell testaments often contained predictions of future crises including the appearance of apostates and impostors (see 1:12-15). The claim that "there will be false teachers among you" (2:1) serves that purpose, but it is more than a mere convention. The prediction identifies the opposition as false teachers whose duplicity meant they would be condemned to death, in line with the provisions of Deut 18:20. Second, the comparison of the teachers with false prophets is consonant with their portrayal as illegitimate teachers who "malign the truth" and "exploit" their adherents.

The author's indictment of the teachers for their greed and deception (v. 3) echoes Jewish moral tradition. The entire phrase "the way of the truth will be maligned" reflects the influence of Isa 52:5 (LXX) "because of you my name is always maligned among the Gentiles" (Kelly 1981, 328; also Bauckham 1983, 242; and see Paul's use of this Isaianic verse in Rom 2:24). Second Tim 2:14-18 and Titus 2:7-8 also express a similar concern that the community show a consistency of life and belief before unbelievers.

The comparison of false teachers with false prophets connects this section to 1:20-21, but it also introduces the major concerns and content of the rest of the letter. The explicit attack on the false teachers begins here, particularly the charges of greed and immorality, which are repeated later (2:14-15; 2:18-19). Second, the author introduces the dispute over the timeliness and nature of God's judgment (2:2; 2:9-10; 3:6, 8-10). Third, the exposure of the opposition as pseudo-teachers whose corrupt ways will lead to their destruction (2:2) continues in the following section (2:3*b*, 10, 12-13, 14, 17, 20-22) as well as in chapter 3 (3:5-7, 16).

Proofs of God's Judgment and Mercy (2:3*b*-10*a*)

Verses 3*b*-10 begin a series of denunciations of the other teachers' positions and behavior. Verse 3*b* pronounces judgment on the false teachers for bringing shame on the faith and manipulating the gospel for their own ends. It also forms a topic sentence for the extended argument found in verses 4-10*a*. Here the author refutes the contention that God does not judge humanity for its behavior.

The argument in 2:3*b*-10 begins with the dual claims that "judgment" has not been idle and that destruction has not been asleep. An extended conditional sentence (vv. 4-9*a*) follows these claims. First mentioned are three illustrations of God's willingness and ability to punish disobedience (disobedient angels, the pre-flood ancient world, and Sodom and Gomorrah; vv. 4, 5*a*, 6). The author weaves two examples of obedient faith into these illustrations: Noah (v. 5*b*) and Lot (vv. 7-8). Both men are "righteous," and both demonstrate that while God punishes the ungodly, God also rescues those who live according to the divine will. The argument concludes with verse 9, where the author states that the evidence drawn from the past (and from Scripture) shows that God "knows how to rescue well-doers from temptation, and how to keep the unrighteous under punishment until the day of judgment." In verse 10, the author applies the argument to his opponents, concluding that God will condemn those who, like the opposition, follow the flesh and despise authority.

◊   ◊   ◊   ◊

Ancient Examples of God's Actions (2:3*b*-6)

The fundamental structure and elements of the argument in verses 4-8 are drawn from Jude 5-7. The most notable differences are: (1) the corrected chronological arrangement, (2) the addition of positive illustrations of righteousness to Jude's portrayals of disobedience, and (3) the elision of the particular sins of the negative exemplars. Jude recounted these examples to show that disobedience would forfeit the believer's positive status before God. Our author presents them as evidence that God has always executed judgment by punishing the ungodly and rescuing the righteous.

The author's first illustration involves the rebellious angels who mated with the women of Earth, taking them as wives (Gen 6:1-4). Unlike Jude, who emphasized the angels' abandonment of their divinely established station, the author of 2 Peter condemns the angels simply because they sinned (see comment on Jude 6). The statement that God did not spare the angels, but cast them into hell is evidence of God's judgment.

The verb *tartarōsas* ("cast into hell") literally means to cast into Tartarus. The verb is unique to 2 Peter in the Greek Bible, but the cognate noun occurs in *1 Enoch* 20:2 where it refers to the place of divine punishment (see Job 40:20 (LXX); Prov 30:16; *Sib. Or.* 4:186; Philo, *Praem.* 152). "Tartarus" was the name for the lowest part of the underworld where, according to classical Greek mythology, Zeus imprisoned the Titans after they were defeated in war. As Neyrey suggests, the author has shaped this example from Genesis so that it recalls the Greek myth in order to produce "an example readily recognized by Greek and Jewish hearers [which] seems calculated to appeal to common knowledge about divine punishment of the wicked" (Neyrey 1993, 202).

According to the author, the angels are imprisoned and "kept until judgment." The phrasing recalls the language of Jude 6 as well as Jude's conceptions of eschatological judgment. Although our author has used Jude's term "kept," it lacks the sense of irony displayed in Jude (see comments on Jude 1 and 6). The author of 2 Peter always uses "kept" with regard to the final judgment (2:4, 9, 17; 3:7). Here, as in the examples that follow, he shows how past instances of judgment prefigure the final eschatological judgment. Sometimes God's verdicts may not be immediately apparent, like those pronounced on the rebellious angels. Other times, as with Noah's contemporaries, they are all too obvious. But visible or not, they occur, and eventually they will include all of creation (3:7).

In verse 5, the author presents a second example of divine

judgment: the deluge brought on the ancient world. This replaces Jude's story of Israel's rebellion after the rescue from Egypt and accords with the biblical chronology of the examples. Genesis recounts that the flood occurred immediately after the angelic "sons of God" mated with human women. The ordering of the account suggests that the transgression of divine-human boundaries was a significant factor in God's decision to destroy Earth's population (Gen 6:5-9). By returning to the biblical order, the author has placed an emphasis on God's actions in distinction from Jude's focus on the disobedience of God's subjects.

With the expression "ancient world" the author suggests a scope for God's judgment that goes well beyond the biblical account. In Genesis, God decides to "blot out from the earth the human beings I have created" along with other living beings, but the earth itself is not destroyed (Gen 6:7). In 2 Peter, God appears to punish the entire created world. The term *kosmos* ("world") refers directly to Noah's contemporaries as the verse's final phrase "the world of the ungodly" suggests. *Kosmos* also can designate the whole creation and while the author does not make the connection explicit here, he is laying the groundwork for his argument that the entire universe comes under God's final judgment (3:6-7).

The description of Noah also introduces a new element into the argument, namely that God rescues the righteous. In contrast to the sinful angels and to his "ungodly" contemporaries, Noah is a "herald of righteousness." Although Noah is also called "righteous" in Genesis 6:9, the biblical account makes no mention that he is a herald. The author probably relied upon a later Jewish tradition which depicts Noah preaching to his neighbors (Josephus, *Ant.* 1.74; *1 Clem.* 7:6; and especially *Sib. Or.* 1:148-198). The author presents the additional details to demonstrate that the heralds of God's truth have always encountered opposition.

The term "righteousness" (*dikaiosynē*) is another favorite of our author, appearing seven times in the letter (see comment on 1:13). Earlier the author used it to characterize Peter's decision to write his farewell testament, but here it refers to proper conduct before God (1:1; 2:21; 3:13) and to people who display upright behavior in their lives (e.g., Noah, 2:5, and Lot 2:7, 8).

Noah is described with the odd phrase, "Noah, the eighth," which the NRSV rightly paraphrases as "Noah, with seven others" (for a similar use of a numeral to represent a set, see 2 Macc 5:27; BDAG, 689). On a literal level, "eight" refers to Noah, his wife, his three sons, and their wives (Gen 8:18; see also 1 Pet 3:20), but the number also carries a symbolic eschatological reference. Among early Christians, the day of Christ's resurrection was associated with the "eighth day" (see *Barn.* 15:8-9). The resurrection represents the inauguration of a new age (1 Cor 15:20; 2 Cor 5:15-17). Thus, "the eighth" refers not only to the number of people God preserved, but also to the surety of eschatological redemption inaugurated in Christ.

The author expands this analogy by depicting the flood as a cataclysmic punishment brought on the ungodly. The term "ungodly," modifying "the ancient world," echoes the same term of Jude 4, while the verb "to bring" recalls 2:1 where the author stated that the false teachers "bring" upon themselves destruction. The flood is thus a harbinger of the final day of judgment. Just as God punished the wrongdoing of the ancients, so he will punish those who presently disobey him.

After the parenthetical remarks about Noah, the author relies on Jude for his third illustration: Sodom and Gomorrah (see the comment on Jude 7). The verb *katekrinen* ("condemned") picks up the reference to the judgment *(krisis)* of angels (v. 4) and anticipates the eschatological day of judgment *(krisis*, 2:9). The author's choice of alliterative terms strengthens the parallel drawn between the examples of the flood and the fire. The "k" sounds of the Greek phrase *(kataklysmon kosmō)* "flood upon the world" are repeated in the phrase that describes the punishment on Sodom and Gomorrah, *katastrophē katekrinen* ("condemned to extinction") (see also Neyrey 1993, 195-199).

The cities of Sodom and Gomorrah were burned to ashes and condemned to extinction. The verb "to reduce to ashes" (BDAG, 1001) occurs only here in the New Testament, though Philo also used it to refer to the destruction of the two cities (*Ebr.* 223).

"Burning" would have been sufficient to describe their punishment, but the author wished to dramatize the magnitude of God's judgment. Just as the entire world was flooded, so Sodom and Gomorrah were reduced to ashes.

The next phrase further sharpens the point: God made Sodom and Gomorrah "an example of what is coming to the ungodly." God's judgment of the two cities was thorough and permanent, but not isolated. Here the author uses Jude 7 but employs stronger terms, exchanging Jude's term "example" *(deigma)* for the more emphatic term *hypodeigma*. God sets Sodom and Gomorrah as a warning example to "the godlessness of the future." The author has his present opponents, the false teachers and their followers, in mind (2:10). Given that God has provided such a dramatic example of his ability to punish ungodliness, their denial of future judgment is all the more condemnable.

◊ ◊ ◊ ◊

The author of 2 Peter distinguishes the present world from the world to come after Christ's *Parousia* (3:13). Noah and his relatives are exemplars of those who will live in the age to come. Because they were faithful to God in adversity, they were saved for the world that existed after the flood. Thus, just as God rescued Noah from a perishing world, so too God delivers those who remain steadfast and resist the overtures of the ungodly. The cities of Sodom and Gomorrah function as anti-types. Their punishment becomes a negative example of the consequences of immoral and ungodly behavior. The contrast is stark: disobedience to the will of God is a sign of disregard for his benevolence, while righteousness is the mark of those who rely on God for their ultimate rescue and delivery.

Lot the Exemplar (2:7-8)

In the midst of his description of Sodom, the author presents Lot as a righteous counterexample, repeating the pattern of Noah and the ancient world. This description, however, goes well beyond that of Noah. The author depicts both as righteous men, but he stresses that Lot endured suffering and torment because of his righteousness. The author contrasts Lot's righteous life (emphasized by the triple use of the term *dikaios*) with the ungodly character of his contemporaries (emphasized by the two-fold description of them as "licentious" and "lawless"). Their fates follow from their conduct: Lot is rescued and the inhabitants of Sodom and Gomorrah are destroyed (v. 6).

◊ ◊ ◊ ◊

The account of Lot's actions in Genesis 19 is much more ambivalent than the presentation in 2 Peter. In Genesis 19, Lot appears only to placate the strangers who visit Sodom, and to have resisted the offensive behavior of his neighbors. Apparently our author follows another strand of Jewish parenesis in which the obedient servant of God resists the overtures of the pagan world (Philo, *Mos.* 2:58; Wis 10:6). In 2 Peter, licentious behavior leaves Lot "greatly distressed," and he is "internally tormented" by his neighbors' lawless deeds. The term "greatly distressed" refers to someone who is oppressed or worn out by constant strain. Lot, living in the midst of immorality, is steadily affronted by it, and resisting it wears him down. The phrases "living among them day after day" and "tormented in his righteous soul by their lawless deeds" express the same idea. Lot's torment is essentially mental rather than physical, a stress felt in his soul as he tries to maintain a righteous life in an unrighteous environment.

◊ ◊ ◊ ◊

The introduction of Noah and Lot as the righteous ones who maintain their faith are the author's attempts to exhort his readers to the same fidelity. The audience lives, as Noah and Lot did, among ungodly people (3:7). Yet Noah and Lot did not abandon their responsibility to God and were rewarded for their faithfulness. The author urges his readers to show the same commitment. Pressured by the "ungodly" teachers (who will suffer the same fate as the ancient tormentors), the readers should remain faithful to God's will. If so, they, like Noah and Lot, will be rescued by God (1:11; 3:8-14, 17-18).

The Proofs Applied (2:9-10a)

Verse 9 makes the hope of deliverance explicit. Its language recalls the terms of verses 4-8: God rescued *(errysato)* Lot (v. 7) and kept *(teroumenous)* the angels for judgment *(eis krisin)* (v. 4). If God delivered Noah and Lot, and if God punished the ungodly, "then the Lord knows how to rescue *(ryesthai)* the godly from trial, and to keep *(terein)* the unrighteous under punishment until the day of judgment" *(kriseōs)*. The term *peirasmos* ("trial") can refer to instances of temptation (e.g. Luke 4:13) but also to trials or tests of probity. Here, the author has in mind Lot's distress rather than the appeal of sin or evil. The phrase "rescue from trial" is best understood in the light of the previous examples of "the afflictions which the righteous suffer in an evil world" (Bauckham 1983, 253; see also Kelly 1981, 335). Lot experienced the pressures of everyday life in the midst of people who did not share his values or commitments. In this sense, he is a paradigm for all people who desire to live righteously in a wicked and hostile environment.

The two parts of the double conclusion stand in sharp contrast. In one case, God rescues the "godly" but, in the other, he "keeps the unrighteous" for "punishment" *(kolazomenous),* i.e., divine retribution (BDAG, 554-555). The syntax of this phrase is uncertain. The NRSV translation, "to keep the unrighteous under punishment until the day of judgment," implies that the punishment occurs now rather than at the eschaton. This accords well with the Greek text and it follows the pattern of verse 4, where the angels presently are kept in chains until the final judgment, as well as the notion of immediate punishment for wrongdoing presented in the previous examples (vv. 4-6).

The difficulty however, is that the conclusion does not appear to apply to the false teachers. They are also unrighteous, but there is no apparent present punishment for their wrongdoing. As a result, the phrase probably should be translated "to hold the unrighteous for punishment on the day of judgment." Admittedly this requires reading the present participle *kolazomenous* with a future sense. This does occur in Koine Greek, however, and the author uses a present participle *lyomenon* ("being loosed") with a future meaning ("will be dissolved") in 3:11.

This translation fits the author's overall argument. One may not see the evidence yet, but the unrighteous have been marked for judgment. Further, the author desired to connect this conclusion to the false teachers in v. 10*a*. Verse 9 thus forms a general conclusion to verses 4-8 and a specific indictment of the opposition. Finally, this translation also is consonant with the author's statement that the present heavens and earth "are being kept" for the day of judgment and the destruction of the ungodly (3:7).

The author applies the conclusion of the proofs to the opposition in verse 10*a*. The false teachers are egregious examples of unrighteous behavior, so the general truth that God will punish the wicked is "especially" true in their case. The superlative adjective *malista* ("especially") underscores that the opponents are "most of all" candidates for God's judgment. The author draws from Jude 7-8 to describe the false teachers as those who indulge their flesh and those who despise authority, but he again modifies the terms. He exchanges Jude's "went after" *(apelthousai opisō)* for a phrase often found in the LXX, "to go after" *(poreuesthai opisō)* which was used to describe Israel's following of false gods (LXX Deut 4:3; 6:14; 28:14). The author likely wanted this echo to be heard, in order to suggest that the flesh has become a god for these people. The next phrase underscores this charge. The opponents indulge in "depraved lust" *(epithymia miasmou)*, literally "in desire of corruption." That is, the false teachers do not simply indulge in the flesh, they actively seek to serve it in defilement.

The next phrase, which the NRSV translates "who despise authority," implies a denial of Christ. The abstract noun *kyriotētos* ("authority") is a cognate of *kyrios* ("lord"), which connects with verse 9 and the charge of 2:1: they will even deny the Master. Instead of desiring righteousness and virtue, the opponents seek pollution and corruption, and although they claim allegiance to God (and Christ), they "go after the flesh" as idolaters.

◊   ◊   ◊   ◊

This section begins with the personification of "judgment" and "destruction" and ends with the claim that God knows how to punish those who deny him. Judgment and destruction (as agents of God) are not unaware of the unrighteous behavior of the opponents, nor are they apathetic toward it. Nor does the lack of direct and immediate action by God mean that God is incapable of acting. The opposition's sentence has already been handed down and it will be executed. As the readers will be reminded, the Lord's slowness to act is not a sign of indifference or inability, but a measure of his patience (3:8-9).

It is most likely that the opponents claimed that only those who ignored reality could believe in a God who passes judgment on evil. The questions that challenge belief in a personal God must have been part of their repertoire: "If God really does judge human actions, then why do we see no evidence of it?" or "Why, if God is a real judge, do the wicked seem unaffected and the good still suffer? Is God sleeping or otherwise occupied?" The author vigorously refutes this line of reasoning. In doing so, he stands in a long tradition of both Jewish and Christian thought that rejects any claim that God slumbers (Ps 121:4; Isa 5:27) or is incapable of acting.

These questions were not original to the opponents in 2 Peter. Israel raised similar questions about competing gods when Elijah mocked Baal's prophets (1 Kgs 18:27) and when God appeared to have abandoned Israel (Ps 44:23). Greek philosophers who denied that the gods were active in the world's affairs also raised these issues (see Introduction). As Neyrey notes, "Epicureans typically denied that the Deity either rewarded or punished, thus acclaiming the inactivity of God (Cicero, *Nat. Deor.* 1.9.51)" (Neyrey 1993, 202).

Although the author's opponents need not have followed the entire philosophic argument, they may have accepted the idea that God was inactive in the world. More to the point, they need not have viewed this as a denial of belief in God, but rather as a logical interpretation of God's actions in Christ, i.e., since redemption had already occurred, God would not revoke it in the future.

Having supplied examples of the Lord's ability to punish and rescue, the author must still demonstrate the flaw in the opponents' thinking as well as explain the "non-occurrence" of the second coming. He undertakes these challenges with the proofs and apologies found in 3:5-7; 8-10.

The Character of the Opponents (2:10*b*-22)

"This indictment [vv. 10*b*-16], with its sequel in 17-22, is the most violent and colorfully expressed tirade in the New Testament" (so Kelly 1981, 337). The author's language and examples are drawn from Jude 8-15, but once again he modifies his source to serve his own purposes. The opposition's errors pertain not only to matters of belief or thought, but also to character and morality. The author therefore indicts them for presumptuous attitudes and destructive actions.

The section is loosely connected by means of catchwords, puns, and innuendo; the apparent connections are more the result of rhetorical flourish than logical flow. The characterizations spill out in a cascade of judgment, and their sheer volume is intended to cause the readers to be repulsed by the teachers they once esteemed. The overall portrait is stunning: the false teachers are not just in error, they are irredeemable, hopelessly corrupt, and a source of pollution in the community. The fact that the author devotes over one third of his letter to their denunciation underscores the depth of his disdain.

For purposes of explanation the denunciations can be divided into two sections: verses 10*b*-16, and verses 17-22. The repetition of the term "these people" (vv. 10*b*, 17) signals a slight break. Throughout the section the author seeks to unmask the true identity of his opponents and the threat they pose both to individual believers and the community as a whole.

The Irrationality of the Opposition (2:10b-16)

The first two words of verse 10*b* sum up the author's basic evaluation of the opposition; they are "bold and willful." Not only are they wrong in their belief, but they arrogantly persist in their error. The examples that follow—the slander of the glorious ones (vv. 10*b*-11), the opposition's irrationality (vv. 12-13), and its insatiable desire for sin (vv. 14-15)—illustrate their ignorant arrogance. Ironically the opposition believes it is free from any future bar of judgment (2:19). By contrast, our author insists that they are already accursed (2:14), self-condemned (2:13), and bound for imprisonment (2:4, 9). Despite their denials, they will indeed face a future judgment.

"Bold" *(tolmētai)* and "willful" *(authadeis)* were often joined in ancient ethical discourse to denote impetuous and ill-advised behavior. In Jude 9, the angel Michael "did not dare" *(etolmē sen)* to pronounce judgment on the devil, thereby slandering him (see comment on Jude 9). The author of 2 Peter does not recount this incident, but he picks up its sentiment with his use of corresponding adjective "bold" *(tolmētai)* and the term "blaspheme/slander" in the next phrase. The second term, "willful," underscores the opposition's headstrong nature.

The false teachers demonstrate their audacity by their lack of fear: they "slander the glorious ones *(doxas)*." This passage is difficult to interpret because the referent of *doxas* is uncertain and the form that the opposition's slander might have taken is unclear. Some interpreters understand "the glorious ones" as human authorities, which allows for a natural use of "they slander." This interpretation places a significant strain on *doxas*, however, especially in light of verse 11. Most likely, *doxas* refers to glorious angelic powers (its meaning in Jude). Even then it is unclear whether the author considered the "glorious ones" to be good or evil.

The thought unit continues into verse 11, and so does the obscurity of the Greek syntax. Literally translated, the verse reads, "whereas angels stronger and more powerful do not bring against them *(kat' autōn)* a slanderous judgment from the Lord." Two questions arise here: (1) Compared to whom are the angels stronger? and (2) Against whom do they refrain from bringing judgment?

If the glorious ones are understood as good angels, then a paraphrase of 11 would be: "the false teachers slander good angels even though they do not enjoy this right, but good angels, stronger and more powerful (than the false teachers), refrain from bringing a charge against them (the teachers) even though their station might permit this." If, however, the "glorious ones" are understood as evil angels, then another logic applies. The opposition slanders evil powers, but even good angels refrain from bringing a charge against the evil powers. In either case, the teachers show their arrogance by overstepping their authority and violating God's natural ordering of reality. Reaching a decision is difficult, but the understanding of "blaspheming" suggested below favors the second alternative.

Matters of interpretation are complicated further because the nature of the blasphemy against the angelic powers is not defined. The actual words or manner of blasphemy can only be conjectured, but it is unlikely that the opposition actually would have slandered beneficent angels. More likely, they showed disdain or disregard for evil powers by denying that these powers could hold sway over them. The opponents may not have understood their disregard for demonic powers as blasphemy. Indeed, they may have considered it a sign of their freedom (2:19), but the author considered it a gross misunderstanding of human and divine relationships.

The arrogance and ignorance displayed by the false teachers cause the author to compare them to "irrational animals" who react but do not think. Hence, "they slander what they do not understand." The disparaging comparison goes beyond their lack of reasoning capacity. According to ancient thought, wild animals were in the world in order to be "captured and killed." The teachers have a similarly predetermined destiny.

Three times the author describes the fates of the wild animals and the teachers with the term *phthora*. The animals are born "to be killed" *(eis phthoran),* and the false teachers' destructive behavior *(phthora)* dictates the manner in which they will be destroyed *(phtharēsontai).* Jude 10 has influenced the author's choice of language, but "destruction/destroyed" *(phthora)* is also one of his favorite terms (1:4, 2:19). Its use here stresses the eschatological fate of the teachers.

The phrase in verse 12, *en tē phthora autōn kai phtharēsontai* (NRSV: "when those creatures are destroyed, they also will be destroyed" or "in their destruction they also will be destroyed"), is, like the phrases in verses 10 and 11, ambiguous. As a result, it can be understood in numerous ways, of which three are viable: the destruction of the false teachers is being compared (1) to that of the animals, (2) to that of the evil angels, or (3) to their own manner of destructive behavior. The alternative one chooses depends on how the pronoun *autōn* ("them") is interpreted. If the author intended a comparison with the animals, then he was suggesting that just as wild animals meet violent and sudden deaths, so the destruction of the false teachers will occur swiftly and as a surprise. This alternative comports well with 2:1. Further, just as the ignorant animals do not know their fate, neither do the false teachers (see Kelly 1981, 339). If, however, the author was comparing the fate of the evil angels with that of the false teachers, then the phrase implies that as the evil powers will experience destruction at the eschatological judgment, so will the false teachers (Bauckham 1983, 264).

Finally, it may be that the author was simply employing a Hebraism for the sake of emphasis. He does something similar in 3:3 where he refers to the latter days when "scoffers will come, scoffing." If so, then the author is implying a type of *lex talionis* (see Neyrey 1993, 209); i.e., the false teachers will suffer destruction commensurate with the destruction they have caused. Thus, the translation would be, "They shall be destroyed with the same destruction they have brought about." This last alternative is attractive because it works well grammatically, follows the logic that the opponents bring about their judgment, and forms a parallel with the next phrase which is also a *lex talionis:* "they will suffer wickedly *(adikoumenoi)* the wages of wickedness *(adikias)*." In this case, verses 12 and 13*a* both refer to the severity of the punishment the opponents will receive, and both show that the punishment is a fit response to their own wicked and destructive behavior.

Verse 13 follows the theme introduced in verse 12. By means of a word play on *adikein*, the author shows that the opposition will suffer wrong *(adikoumenoi)* for the wrong *(adikias)* they have done. The NRSV translation of verse 13: "suffering the penalty for wrongdoing" does not reflect the poetry of the author's pun. The repetition of the terms recalls the reference to God's judgment of the unrighteous *(adikous*, v. 9) who are "kept in judgment" while also foreshadowing the indictment of the teachers for following Balaam, who "loved the wages of doing wrong" *(adikias*, v. 15).

In the latter part of verse 13, the author refers to the opposing teachers as *spiloi* and *mōmoi*, "blots and blemishes." The first of these terms is close to Jude's "stains/reefs" *(spilades)* and was probably suggested by that text (Jude 12). Since Jude's use of *spilades* likely would have been opaque to the audience of 2 Peter, the author adopted the similar word *spiloi* to show that the opposition's presence pollutes the community. The teachers are only spots and blemishes on God's people, not really a part of them. The author will make this differentiation plain in the next chapter when he exhorts the readers to strive "to be found by him [God] at peace, without spot or blemish" (3:14).

The author brackets his charges with indictments of the opposition for "reveling in the daytime" and for corrupting the community's agape meals. The term "revel" can convey the positive sense of "delighting in something." Usually, however, it connotes self-indulgent behavior, often in connection with drunken rowdiness. Most revelers restrict their drinking to the cover of darkness, but the shameless opposition revels in broad daylight. The opposition is actually doubly condemned: first for indulgent behavior and then for displaying no sense of shame. Such hyperbole was standard fare in ancient polemic (see Bauckham 1983, 265), so it is not certain that the false teachers were public drunks. The rhetoric, however, does show the author's disdain for the teachers and emphasizes his contention that false doctrine leads to a life of blatant immorality.

Even more damnable than the opponents' reveling is their

behavior that reduces the community's agape feasts to orgiastic banqueting. The term "to feast together" is taken from Jude 12 where Jude's opponents were accused of invading the church's fellowship meals. The phrase "while they feast with you" would have evoked images of the eucharaist/agape meal. But these feasts can no longer be agape meals, because the presence of the heretical teachers transforms the addressees' *agapais* ("love feasts") into *apatais* ("riotous banquets"). The message is clear: the mere presence of these teachers in the community's worship destroys its sacral nature. Hence even to entertain the false teachers at the agape feast puts the community at risk.

The litany of complaints continues with the next participial phrase, which charges the false teachers with a complete lack of self-control. Their desire for sin is so insatiable that women are viewed purely as opportunities to commit adultery. The opponents view no one (community members included) as a fellow believer but only as an opportunity to fulfill base desires. Not only do the false teachers exploit people for their own gain (2:3); they "entice" them. This verb literally means "to dangle bait before a fish," so this expression charges the opponents with "trolling" for unsteady souls, preying on those whose firmness in the faith has not yet developed (see 1:12).

Finally, in contrast to the "unsteady ones," the opposition has been thoroughly schooled, only not in faith, but in the art of rapacity. Rather than being "established in the truth" as God's people (1:12), they have "hearts trained in greed." They are driven only by avarice, a charge already leveled at 2:3. Again, the author underscores the inevitability of judgment. They are "accursed children" (a Semitic expression), i.e., they live under the curse of God, analogous to "children of transgression" (Isa 57:4) or "children of wrath" (Eph 2:3). Even though they do not conceive of the possibility of their judgment, the author insists that it has already been pronounced. The charge thus recalls 2:3 and looks ahead to 2:21-22 where the author insists that they have turned back "from the holy commandment."

Verse 15 continues the charge of greediness, comparing the

false teachers to Balaam, "son of Bosor." This epithet is found nowhere else in antiquity, and some manuscripts have corrected the reading to "Beor," the name of Balaam's father found in Num 22:5 (LXX). Still, *Bosor* has strong manuscript support, and this, combined with the rarity of the name, suggests that it is the original and correct reading. The unusual form reflects a word play on the Hebrew term for "flesh" *(basar)*: by employing it, the author was calling Balaam a "son of flesh" (Bauckham 1983, 267-268). Like the "child of flesh," the opposition is defined by its desires for the flesh (2:13, 14, 18). Like Balaam, the opposition came pretending to offer oracles from God, and like Balaam, they are corrupt because they are motivated by profiting from wickedness (Jude 11).

According to the author, Balaam "loved the wages of doing wrong." This phrase is a reference to later Jewish interpretations of Numbers 22–24 (see comment on Jude 11) that depict Balaam giving advice to Balak, king of Moab, to tempt the men of Israel by placing beautiful women before them. Balaam was paid for this and is charged with betraying the people of Israel for monetary gain. This tradition is useful to the author since he has just charged his opponents with "enticing unsteady souls" (2:14) and following the path of Balaam by tempting the people of God to sin. Likewise, they follow Balaam as "prophets" who are motivated by their greed rather than by the truth.

Just as Balaam was "rebuked for his transgression," so the false teachers will be judged for theirs. Here the author amplifies Jude and includes the tradition of Balaam's rebuke by a "dumb animal" (Num 22:21-35). In antiquity, animals were considered mute, not because they were unable to make sounds, but because they could not speak a language. Thus when the author makes reference to the "human voice," he is suggesting that the uttered rebuke ultimately came from God's intervention. The author probably was relying on a later Jewish interpretation of the biblical story, since in Numbers it is an angel and not the donkey that upbraids Balaam (see Bauckham 1983, 268, for reference to the Targumic interpretations).

This tradition would account for the author's reference to

Balaam's "madness" *(paraphronian)*, which was also stressed in the Jewish traditions (cf. Philo, *Mut.* 203 and *Mos.* 1.293). The term, unique to 2 Peter, creates a word play with *paranomias* ("transgression," v. 16), linking Balaam's madness with his behavior, something the author also wished to do with the false teachers' words and actions. Balaam's attempt to deceive Israel and his acceptance of payment for his efforts were not only transgressions; they were acts of pure folly. The illustration imputes the same madness to the opposition.

The Final Status of the Opposition (2:17-22)

The author reiterates the polemic of verses 10*b*-15 in verses 17-22, noting again that the opponents entice people to sin (2:14, 2:18) and repeating the charge that the opponents are departing from the way *(hodos)* of righteousness (2:21; cf. 2:15). Finally, he points out once more that, despite their belief to the contrary, the opponents will suffer judgment (see 2:4, 9, 13, 17).

The author presents his fundamental charge against the opponents in verse 19: the opponents promise freedom when they are actually re-instituting bondage. Because they promise release from all restraint, the opponents are teaching "bombastic nonsense," that leads the audience to the error from which they had escaped. The author expresses this tragedy with a collection of proverbial material that brings this section to a climax.

◊ ◊ ◊ ◊

Verses 17 and 18 describe the true nature of the opposition and their teaching. Returning to the imagery (but not the exact language) of Jude once more, the author refers to the false teachers as "waterless springs" and "mists driven by a storm." In the first image the author substitutes the term *pegai* ("springs") for Jude's "clouds." Although they appear to offer exactly what the believer needs and desires, the opponents are like dried up springs providing only the *appearance* of being able to quench spiritual thirst.

The opponents' teaching disappoints because it provides only illusory and hollow forms of the truth. The next image, which depicts them as "mists driven by a storm," underscores this emptiness. These mists are the haze "which is left after the condensation of cloud into rain" (Kelly 1981, 345). Ephemeral and empty mists can provide no relief from drought. Likewise, there is not enough substance in the new teaching to sustain a believer's spiritual life. Like the mists, the teaching has no real weight or depth and evaporates under the heat of scrutiny.

In contrast to the flimsy and transient nature of the opponents' teaching, a permanent and final punishment awaits them. The phrase "for them the deepest darkness has been reserved" is drawn verbatim from Jude 13 (see comment). The metaphor of the "deep darkness" is an apt image for eschatological judgment and punishment. The teachers are superficial, their promises are hollow and fleeting, but the punishment that awaits them is severe and everlasting (cf. 2:4).

Three additional charges broaden the exposé of the opponents' teaching in verse 18: (1) the teachers prey on recent converts, (2) they tempt their listeners to participate in licentious behavior, and (3) their teaching is "bombastic nonsense." The last phrase is an oxymoron (lit. "puffed-up emptiness") and asserts once more the opponents' vacuity. Despite their impressive sound, their words are void of content. The charge of enticing with "licentious desires of the flesh" "those who have just escaped" recalls the general charge made in 2:14: "they entice unsteady souls." The repetition of the word *deleazousin* ("entice") emphasizes the attempt to lure the unsuspecting. This time, however, the bait is described as the "desires of the flesh" (see 2:2, 10*a*).

It is unlikely that the false teachers told their listeners to indulge in carnal passions. The teachers more probably were confusing their listeners about what moral conduct was appropriate to Christian believers. The author has cast their teaching in the most negative terms in order to distinguish clearly between the moral conduct of the believing community and the behavior of the outside world. But the fact that he was attempting to do so shows how unclear this distinction had actually been.

The author's expression, "those who have just (barely) escaped," refers either to those who have recently entered the community (i.e., "barely" as a temporal term), or to those who are still oriented to their former lives (i.e., still coming to accept the belief and conduct of the Christian life). In either case, these people represent the most vulnerable members of the community and the author is outraged that they were the target of the opponents.

Verse 19 continues the thought initiated in verse 18. The opposition entices the recent converts by promising them freedom, which is an appeal with "deep attraction and ambiguity" (Bauckham 1983, 275). The author's phrasing sarcastically employs a catchword from the opposition ("freedom"). How, he asks, can one believe the claims of teachers whose own teaching returns them to their former life of error? Thus, he taunts them in asking, "How can you promise freedom when you are slaves of desires?"

The nature of the promised freedom, however, is left undefined. Early Christian writers often understood freedom *(eleutheria)* as release from the power of sin and death (2 Cor 3:17; Gal 2:4; 5:1, 13; Rom 6:18), but since this meaning would have been part of traditional Christian preaching and teaching, the opposition must have meant something else. Commentators have suggested four possibilities: (1) freedom from socially constructed moral constraint, (2) a Gnostic notion that freedom is release from cosmic powers, (3) freedom from corruption *(phthora),* or (4) freedom from fear of judgment. The Gnostic thought is unlikely since the author displays no evidence of this type of duality, but the other three are all viable options.

It may have been that the teachers advocated something like the libertinism Paul combats in 1 Corinthians (see also Rom 3:8, 6:1-4; Gal 5:13). If so, they would have argued that since believers are free in Christ, they are free from all societal constraints. Since this age is passing away, conventional rules and laws do not pertain to the eschatological people of God (1 Cor 7:29-31). Further, since God saves human beings through the beneficence of grace, moral codes do not apply to those in believe in Christ. Three features of the letter support this possibility. First, the author does charge his opposition with taking an anti-law stance

(2:7, 8, 10, 21). Second, 1 Pet 2:16 implies similar charges, and in some fashion 2 Peter presupposes this letter (see comment on 3:1-2). Third, the reference to Paul's letters in 3:15-16 could refer to the misinterpretation of Paul's arguments about God's grace.

Options 3 and 4 are fundamentally related to the opponents' denial of future judgment (2:3*b*, 10). If the false teachers promised their listeners freedom from final divine punishment, they also promised freedom from any fear the prospect of judgment might have produced. Option 3 involves another variation. The teachers may have claimed that Christians, who had been saved by God, were already transformed and hence were no longer subject to the corruption of mortality (see, e.g., 1 Cor 15:42-49). Thus, Christians were living an eschatological existence already and, in effect, they were free from future judgment.

It is quite likely that an amalgam of these options characterized the opposition's teaching. As an eschatological people, Christians could claim "new existence" and freedom from the world's moral standards as well as freedom from a future judgment of the world. The teachers could have understood their position as a natural extension of belief in a new creation, and argued that, since God has set Christians free from sin and the temptations of the world, their freedom in Christ is absolute. Moreover, even if God will judge the world in the future, Christians have already been redeemed by Christ's sacrifice (see 1 Pet 1:18-19, 2:24). Thus, Christians should realize that they are free from this world's power and from worry about their status in the world to come.

The author believed that although they were unaware of it, the opponents were really "slaves of corruption." Their fundamental misunderstanding of judgment has condemned them (2:1-3, 12-13). The author used *phthora* ("corruption") to suggest both moral overtones (i.e., the teachers are under the control of worldly passion) and eschatological judgment (1:4; 2:12). Since the teachers are under the control of *moral* corruption (2:20) they will also suffer *eschatological* destruction (2:12).

The phrase "for whoever is overcome by something/someone, is a slave to 'it/him' " was a common proverb in ancient philosophical thought. The relative pronoun *hō* could refer either to a person or a power, but the context suggests a personification of corruption similar to the personification of condemnation in 2:3. The proverb itself refers to conquerors who enslave their enemies after defeating them in battle. Here, the victor is "corruption" *(phthora)*. Defeated by their desires, the teachers forfeit their redeemed state.

The verses that follow depict the reversal of existence from salvation to destruction. One single thought is expressed three times, each time by a proverbial saying. The author is convinced that abandoning the truth is worse than never having known it. A believer, having partaken of the divine nature (1:4), cannot return to a prior existence without penalty. The author allows that judgment may come on the ignorant, but the believer is doubly culpable because he or she claims to have known the truth. Thus, returning to the "defilements of the world" means defying God's judgment and disdaining the gift of freedom from the world's entrapment.

This section repeats the language of 1:3-4 (e.g., "knowledge," 1:3, 2:20; "promise," 1:4, 2:19; "escape," 1:4, 2:20; "corruption in the world," 1:4; "defilements of the world," 2:20). At the beginning of the letter, the author described redeemed existence. Now he describes the state of those who renounced this existence (2:20-22). Tragically having "escaped the defilements of the world through the knowledge of our Lord and Savior Jesus Christ" (see comments on 1:2, 1:4), they have returned to their prior existence and become "entangled" and "overpowered" (a repetition of *hēttaomai* from 2:19) by fleshly desires.

In the end, the last state has become worse for them than the first. Declarations like this understanding of apostasy are found elsewhere in the New Testament (e.g., Heb 6:4-8, 10:26). The expression used here repeats almost word for word a saying attributed to Jesus concerning the fate of a man who, having been exorcised, allowed the unclean spirit to return (Matt 12:45 par. Luke 11:26). Jesus pronounces that his last state would be worse than his initial possession because his demon would return, bringing seven more with him. The fact that our author expresses the same thought shows how seriously early Christians took this matter and perhaps how widespread the problem of reversion was among early converts.

The statements about apostasy are reiterated in verses 21-22 by two maxims: a *Tobspruch*, i.e., a saying of Hebrew wisdom that follows the pattern "It is better to . . . than to . . ." (see Snyder 1977, 119) and "a true proverb." Both sayings graphically portray the nature of those who reject their God-given status and return to their prior unclean state.

In verse 21, the Christian life is called "the way of righteousness," picking up language used earlier in the chapter ("way," 2:2, 15; "righteousness," 2:5). The deliberate terminology contrasts the initial state of conversion ("to have known the way of righteousness," as expressed in 1:2, 3) with the choice the false teachers have made, i.e., "to forsake the right way and follow the way of Balaam" (2:15). Apostasy is further defined as "to turn back from the holy commandment." The expression is a parallel to the "way of righteousness," and the author had no particular commandment in mind. Rather, he is describing the Christian ethic as a commandment (3:2) much like the Jewish law could be called "the commandment of Moses" (Rom 7:8-12; Heb 7:18; see also John 14:12).

In verse 22, the author cites two more proverbs in parallel form and calls them "the true proverb." Most likely he has found them already coupled in a Hellenistic Jewish wisdom collection and has adopted them for his purposes here (so Bauckham 1991, 279). The use of two aphorisms about "unclean animals" is a fitting way to end a polemic that began with a charge that "these (false teachers) are like irrational animals" (2:12). Jews considered both dogs and pigs unclean and despicable (e.g., Matt 7:6). The earlier collector of the proverbs likely drew the first aphorism from Prov 26:11, "Like a dog that returns to its vomit is a fool who reverts to his folly." The second has no biblical parallel, but it is similar to the imagery in the *Story of Ahikar*. In the Syriac version of this tale a father says, "You were to me, my son, like a swine which had had a bath, and when it saw a slimy pit went down and bathed in it" (8:18). Both proverbs make the point that, by their nature, pigs and dogs when cleaned do not remain clean, but always return to the filth that defines them. The comparison of the opposition to unclean animals shows the base and irrational nature of their actions.

◊   ◊   ◊   ◊

The phrasing in verses 20-22 leaves unclear whether it is the apostates who are the false teachers or their followers since either group can serve as the antecedent of the pronoun "they" (v. 20). In the end, however, it seems likely that the primary referents are the false teachers, since the entire chapter has been aimed at them. Even if the rebuke was aimed at the false teachers, however, those who were attracted to their teaching surely heard it. Thus, the characterization of the opposition as apostates destined for destruction warns the "unsteady souls" enticed by the false teachers. The author does not directly address them, but they were surely in mind when he wrote. By exposing the polluting force of the false teachers, he warns his readers that agreeing to the "false" teachings would mean that they, too, stood in danger of apostasy. Thus, the chapter serves the dual purpose of attacking the false teachers and warning the rest of the community, especially recent converts. It was crucial that the author show his readers the true nature of the teachers' positions, because what may have appeared as a reasonable alternative to initial Christian instruction turns out to be the severest form of apostasy from it.

Peter's Reminder (3:1-4)

Having completed the polemic that revealed the errorists' true character, the author returns to the testament genre initiated at 1:12-15. He has shown that the opponents did not have a proper understanding of truth and that they were morally bankrupt. Now he repeats one of the letter's main concerns: the integration of proper belief with sound ethics and strong morals (1:5; 2:17-18). In the first part of the chapter he will deal with correct thinking, turning to correct behavior at the end (3:11-13; 14-18).

◊ ◊ ◊ ◊

Verses 1 and 2 connect this section to other portions of the letter by their language and by reintroducing motifs from the farewell discourse genre. The use of *hypomnēsei* ("arouse") in verse 1 and *mnēsthēnai* ("to remember") in verse 2 recall the language of reminder used in 1:12-15. By referring to the dual authority of the holy prophets and apostolic witness, the author calls to mind the material in 1:16-18 (the revelation to the apostles) and 1:19-21 (the inspired truth of prophecy).

The author refers to the present letter as the "second epistle" "Peter" has written to the audience for this purpose. The reference to a "second epistle" causes speculation about the identity of a first letter, which most interpreters take to be 1 Peter (e.g., Kelly 1981, 352; Bauckham 1983, 286). Some commentators reject this possibility due to the dissimilar contents of the two letters. Accordingly, they have proposed three main alternatives: (1) Jude; (2) a portion of 2 Peter, usually chapters 1 and 3; and (3) an epistle now lost to us.

The first option is consistent with the fact that the author used Jude as a source, but it is an unlikely option. The modifications are atypical for someone using his own material. Moreover, Jude is not presented as a "reminder," but as a warning and exhortation against disobedience. The second option also is unlikely, because 3:2 borrows its language and ideas from 1:13 and because the borrowing from Jude in chapters 1 and 2 continues in chapter 3 as well. The third option is also difficult, since one must conjecture that the author was referring to a letter that is now lost. While possible, this option is unlikely, and the postulation of another Petrine letter only complicates matters.

The major objection to accepting 1 Peter as the previous letter is its scant treatment of the second coming of Christ (only 4:7). The focus of 2 Pet 3:1-2, however, is not primarily teaching about the return of Christ, but the ethical demands prompted by that event. 1 Peter does contain similar exhortations (1:13-17; 1:22-2:1; 2:11-12; 4:3-5, 7-11, 17; 5:4). Thus, even though there are disparities between the two letters, we should conclude that the author of 2 Peter here refers to 1 Peter.

According to the author, the goal of both letters was "to arouse your [the readers'] sincere intention" by reminding them of past proclamations. The collocation of *dianoia* ("mind") and *eilikrinē* ("sincere") requires comment. The first term typically denoted the mind or intelligence (e.g., Mark 12:30; *1 Clem.* 19:3), but in this verse it takes the meaning "disposition" or "thought." The adjective *eilikrinē* (only here in New Testament) modifies *dianoia* creating the idea of "unmixed or pure thought" (NRSV: "sincere intention"). This phrase implies that the believers' thought is not only logically clear, but also morally pure. The believers' thought process has not been corrupted by immoral behavior, which distinguishes them from the opponents (vv. 3-4).

The congregation is to "remember" two things: "the words spoken in the past by the holy prophets" and "the commandment of the Lord and Savior spoken through your apostles." When it does, it will realize that other authoritative voices support the truth of "Peter's" admonitions. The language of prophecy refers here, as it did in 1:19-21, to the Old Testament prophets, specifically to the prophetic words that predicted future judgment.

The second phrase, "the commandment of the Lord and Savior spoken through your apostles," requires more comment. We must consider how the term "commandment" is used; how the double possessive "of the Lord, of the apostles" functions; and what the author intended by the phrase "your apostles." The author previously used "commandment" in 2:21, where the "holy commandment" mirrored the phrase "the way of righteousness" and referred to a mode of conduct (see comment on 2:21). A similar conception of the Christian life appears here, and in this sense, verse 2 recapitulates the epistle's fundamental argument. Rather than listen to "false prophets" and their "secretly destructive opinions" (2:1-3), the audience should recall and rely upon the words of the "holy prophets" and the ethical command of Christ.

The Greek grammar suggests that the commandment belongs *both* to the apostles *and* to the Lord. The expression is awkward, but the author must mean that the apostles proclaimed a commandment given to them by Christ. Hence, it is "the Lord's" because it came from him, but it is the apostles' because they transmitted it.

Since the writer uses "I" and "us" whenever he refers to any teaching or revelation that "Peter" or the other apostles received (1:1, 14, 16, 19), one would expect the use of "us" rather than "your apostles" here. It is possible that the phrase does not mean all the apostles but only those who were instrumental in founding and nurturing the congregation. The apostle Peter might not have been one of these apostles, thus the reference to "your apostles." Most likely the phrase is a reference to the initial twelve apostles, and the use of "your" distinguishes the true apostles from the false teachers (so also Bigg 1961, 290). Rather than listen to the false teachers (2:1), the audience should heed the true teaching of Christ's commandment delivered by *their own* apostles.

Verse 3 emphasizes that this is of paramount importance and the key to understanding the present circumstances (as stated in 2:1). The phrase "first of all you must understand this," which repeats the language employed at 1:20, signals this emphasis. Remembering the prophetic prediction enables the audience to recognize what the author knows: the "other teachers" are actually "the false prophets." The author has borrowed this material from Jude 18, but replaced Jude's more unusual phrase "in the last time" with the more familiar "in the last days." In many Old Testament passages, "last day" connotes a future final age when the Lord will reward good and punish evil (Ezek 38:16; Hos 3:5; Mic 4:1). New Testament writers employed it to designate either the final period inaugurated by Christ's death and resurrection (Acts 2:17; 1 Pet 1:20) or the time immediately prior to his return (2 Tim 3:1; Jas 5:3; 1 Pet 1:5). Identifying his own time with the last days permits the author to prove that the predictions in Peter's "farewell testament" are true and that the adversaries have now appeared. The eschatological judgment cannot be far off, since the scoffers own appearance proves that the "last days" have arrived.

The author also borrows the labeling of his opposition as "scoffers" *(empaiktai)* [who] "will come scoffing" *(en empaigmonē)* from Jude 18 (see comment). The coupling of the noun with its cognate verb is a Hebraism that emphasizes the opposition's fundamental identity: scorners of God's truth. Marked both by arrogant teaching and moral deficiency, they reject God's revelation, and, instead of obeying him, "indulge in their own lusts" (see comment on Jude 18). Once again the author insists that false belief and immoral behavior are necessary corollaries. A desire to "indulge in one's own lusts" motivates the opposition's "scoffing," and its immoral behavior indicates that it neither accepts nor understands the truth of Christ's return in judgment (1:4, 2:10, 2:18).

The scoffers deny that Christ will return and mock those who hold this belief. Verse 4 shows that the problem is the non-fulfillment of the promise of Christ's return. Early Christians understood that Christ would return before the apostolic generation had passed away, deriving this belief from Jesus' own predictions (Matt 10:23; Mark 9:1; 13:30; Luke 21:32). Since no return had occurred, the scoffers ask, "where is the promise of his coming?" In Old Testament narratives, questions of this sort often expressed skepticism toward those who continued to hold unrealized beliefs (Pss 42:3, 10; 78:10). Jeremiah 17:15 and Mal 2:17 are especially pertinent, since they reflect the same objections to divine intervention that the author attributes to the scoffers. Jeremiah's audience derides him because his prophecies were not fulfilled. Malachi's mockers point out that there is no evidence that God has or ever will punish evil. A similar tone occurs in the scoffers' question. From their perspective, belief in a future judgment is not simply erroneous; it borders on the ludicrous.

Verse 4 reports the scoffers' main objections: the predicted time frame for the return of Christ has long passed, and there is no observable difference in the world's affairs. The Greek syntax is difficult, but Bauckham's rendering conveys its sense: "For since the fathers fell asleep, everything remains just as it has been since the beginning of the world" (Bauckham 1983, 282). The formulation suggests that the opponents' arguments were made on two levels: the veracity of early Christian beliefs and formal philosophical arguments. On the first level, the non-occurrence of the second coming rendered further belief in it untenable. On the second, future judgment is ruled out categorically because God, by nature, does not intervene in the course of history and because after death there is nothing.

Christian writers often used the phrase "our fathers" (NRSV: "our ancestors") to designate seminal figures from Israel's history (e.g., John 6:31, Rom 9:5, Heb 1:1, *Barn.* 5:7), but in the present context, the expression refers more generally to the first generation of believers. By the time 2 Peter was written, these believers had likely died. Since Jesus had promised to return during that generation's lifetime, their death called into question the validity of his promises. The opposition therefore argued that the second coming of Christ would not occur, since the predicted time for the event had already passed.

The author actually strengthens the opposition's arguments by including the term "for ever since," which extends the time frame of non-occurrence. The force of their objection thus becomes "More than sufficient time has elapsed beyond the promised time frame to conclude that nothing will happen. With the elapse of this much time, we cannot hold this belief." The logic of the argument is sufficiently strong to require a thorough rejoinder, which the author presents in verses 8-9.

The initial objection of the scoffers is based on empirical evidence; i.e., the promised return of Christ has not occurred. Their second objection results from a broader philosophical understanding that the world is immutable and constant. The opposition held that the order and patterns of the natural world prove its constancy and permanent structure. Accordingly, they denied the occurrence of any future cosmic disruption or catastrophic judgment. Thus, on both philosophical and historical grounds, they denied that God could or would intervene in the course of human and natural history.

◊ ◊ ◊ ◊

The section repeats the injunction already expressed earlier to beware of the corrupting opposition. Strains of Epicurean philosophy provide a close analogy to the scoffers' position, particularly the idea that achieving a state of "pleasure" comprised the highest goal of human existence. By "pleasure" Epicureans meant a life free of actions or interactions that could cause trouble, pain, or agitation. Since a constant state of pleasure was the ideal, the Deity, by extension, would also be expected to avoid any actions that caused pain, fear, or trouble, either for itself or for any other being. Diogenes Laertius illustrates this well: "The blessed and eternal being has no trouble himself and brings no trouble upon any other being; hence he is exempt from movements of anger and kindness" (*Diog. Laert.* 10.139, quoted in Neyrey 1993, 123). If they shared these notions, then the opposition would have drawn two conclusions. First, by nature, the Divine would not intervene in the world. Second, since God does not enter into human affairs, there is no reason to anticipate a future judgment by God.

Epicurean thought also held that at death human beings ceased to exist; hence, they need not fear death nor worry about future states of being. Accordingly, life here and now is all that human beings will experience, so again, the idea of a judgment after death is meaningless.

Even if the scoffers' position was similar to Epicurean reasoning, they need not have been Epicureans or followers of their theology (contra Neyrey 1993, 122). Nevertheless, they do appear to have shared the Epicurean skepticism about divine intervention and its position that the human is a free moral agent (2:19). Moreover, they likely argued that virtue is its own reward and needs no motivation by a fear of judgment after death. The author considered that these heretical ideas would lead to immorality (3:3). Still, the opponents' skepticism concerning future judgment could have appealed to many new converts, and the author needed to present sufficient counter-arguments against them.

Replies to the Opposition's Objections (3:5-10)

Throughout the letter, the author has maintained that the opposition's errors reveal their profound ignorance (2:10, 12, 15, 20, 22; 3:16), will lead to destruction (3:7), prove they are dismissive of authority (2:10, 12), and have turned away from righteousness (2:21). Hence, their understanding of God's will and revelation, their discernment of evidence gleaned from history, and their interpretation of the scripture and the prophetic witness are intrinsically and deeply flawed.

In this section, the author presents two "meta-arguments" that engage the opposition's claims and reveal that their entire interpretive framework is defective. In verses 5-7, he demonstrates that a future judgment is consonant with God's pattern of action in the created world. Then, having demonstrated that the second coming can occur, he explains in verses 8-9 why God has delayed Christ's return. The argument culminates with a warning that God's reasons for holding the second coming in abeyance guarantee that it will occur.

◊ ◊ ◊ ◊

First Reply (3:5-7)

The argument in verses 5-7 is based on two axioms; one confirms the opposition's position, and the other refutes it. The author agrees that since God is consistent in dealing with the created world, the past provides a pattern by which one can anticipate the future. He also holds, however, that the historical pattern is one of creation, followed by human disobedience, which results in divine retribution. Hence, in the end, he disagrees with his opponents and argues that they have misinterpreted the historical pattern and therefore draw false inferences from it.

The scoffers' reference to the constancy of creation (v. 4) prompts the author to recount God's creating activity and to reflect on the history of the ancient world. Not only did "the word of God" bring the first heavens and the earth into existence

(v. 5), it also was the instrument by which that world was judged and destroyed (v. 6). The opponents should recognize that while the universe displays a clear pattern of creation, history also shows a pattern of judgment and restoration. This pattern reveals that, by his word, God created the world and destroyed it (v. 6), and with that same word God will bring judgment on the world created after the flood (v. 6-7).

◊ ◊ ◊ ◊

The general outline of the argument in verses 5-7 is obvious, but "it is beset with grammatical, exegetical, and syntactical difficulties . . ." (Kelly 1981, 357). The first of these difficulties appears in the opening phrase of verse 5. The Greek formulation can be translated either as "They deliberately ignore this fact" (NRSV) or as "in maintaining this, they overlook the fact . . ." (NEB). The first option focuses on the will of the opposition, the second on their epistemological error. The position of the word "this" *(touto)* favors the second option, but the first fits the author's charge that the opponents arrogantly choose to ignore facts (2:10, 12, 18, 21-22; 3:16). Either rendering is possible, but given the author's tendency to attribute malevolent motives to his opposition, one might favor the NRSV translation. In this case, the opposition does not inadvertently overlook the truth, but deliberately ignores it. This indictment also demonstrates that, in contrast to the scoffers who ignore or forget the truth, the author constantly reminds the readers of it (1:13-15; 3:1-3). While the scoffers misunderstand history and the word of God, he rightly interprets it (Neyrey 1993, 234).

In the next step of his argument, the author notes that the heavens and earth that "existed long ago" were "formed out of water" "by the word of God." Despite its awkward placement in the Greek sentence, the adverb "long ago" refers to both heaven and earth. The author refers to the world that existed before the flood. The phrases "by the word of God" and "out of water" reflect the author's reliance on Genesis, which describes God forming the heavens and the earth out of the chaotic waters by his word (Gen 1:1-9). The author, however, goes beyond the Genesis account in stating that God creates "by means of water." This amplified phrasing is rather unclear, but the author probably intended to suggest that God fashioned the heavens and the earth by separating the created waters.

The grammar of verse 6 presents still other difficulties. First, it is unclear to what the phrase "through *which* (plural) the world was deluged" refers. Of the numerous possibilities suggested, two seem most probable: the water just mentioned or both the water *(hydōr)* and the word of God *(logos tou theou)* (see Bauckham 1983, 298 for a complete list of the alternatives). If "through which" *(di' hōn)* refers only to the waters of verse 5, this makes the use of the term water in verse 6 redundant. If, on the other hand, "through which" refers to the dual means of destruction, then the author has balanced the two agents of creation in verse 5 (word and water) and the two agents of destruction in verse 6 (word and water) (see Bigg 1961, 293; Kelly 1981, 360). This same idea recurs in verse 7 when the author notes that God will use dual instruments of destruction (word and fire) to judge the present world.

It is also unclear whether "the world of that time" (v. 6) refers to the entire physical world or merely to its inhabitants. The prior references to "the heavens and earth" (vv. 5, 7), where the writer clearly had the physical universe in mind, favor the natural universe. The use of "world" (v. 6) as a collective term referring to both heavens and earth also favors this first possibility. In this case, the destruction of the *"then* world" is parallel to the future destruction of "the *present* heavens and earth" (v. 7). The fact that *kosmos* ("world") often denoted human society (as it does in 2:5*a*) supports the second possibility. Since the author's main argument centers on judgment and not cosmology, "the world of that time" could be a reference to the social order and inhabitants of the earth. In this case, the author is creating a parallel between the ones who perished in the ancient world and the "ungodly" of the present world (v. 6) who will be destroyed in the future (v. 7). A choice is difficult, and perhaps both senses were intended (see Bauckham 1983, 299).

The language of verse 6 is drawn from the flood story of Genesis 7 (see already 2:5), but the thought goes beyond that narrative. The Genesis account refers to the destruction of earth's inhabitants, but not to a total destruction of the planet. Jewish apocalyptic thought had transformed the idea of a flood that destroyed the inhabitants of earth into a total cataclysm that would consume the entire created order (see *1 Enoch* 83:3-5). Our author appears to follow this line of thought, envisioning the destruction as universal.

The final part of verse 6 states that the world was deluged by water and perished, recalling Gen 7:17-24. The first verb "deluged" occurs only here in the New Testament (BDAG, 518), but is also used in Wis 10:4 with reference to the Genesis flood. The second verb, *apōleto* ("perished"), foreshadows the use of the noun *apōleias* ("destruction") in verse 7. In addition, the expression "by water," which describes the means of destruction, is analogous to the use of "by fire" in verse 7. Just as the former world experienced judgment by water, so the present world will experience it by fire.

Verse 7 brings the first argument to a close. The author has shown the legitimacy of interpreting the future in light of the past and has established that the past included judgment as well as creation. He therefore concludes that the pattern of creation/judgment must hold for the future. Since by his word God created the pre-flood world (v. 5) and since by that word the "then" cosmos was destroyed (v. 6), "by the *same* word" (the adjective is emphatic) the "present" heavens and earth are "reserved" for a punishment of fire. The distinction among created orders shows that the author divided history into three epochs. In an initial period, the world was created from the primeval waters and then destroyed by those same waters. In the second post-deluge epoch, the present world was established, and it is destined to end with destruction by fire. Finally, in the third and final epoch, a new eternal creation (1:11) and a place where righteousness dwells (3:13) will replace the present world.

Second Peter is the only New Testament document to suggest that the present world will be destroyed by fire, but the idea also appears in Josephus (*Ant.* 1.70) and in Jewish apocalyptic material (e.g. *Sib. Or.* 2:187-213, 3:83-92, 4:173-181; 1QH 3:29-36). This material builds on Old Testament texts that speak of fire as one of God's instruments of punishment (e.g., Deut 32:22; Ps. 97:3; Isa 66:15-16; Mal 3:19). The apocalyptic material reframes those texts and expands them from a localized judgment into a universal one. Again the author has adopted the apocalyptic eschatological view from these traditions.

The idea of a cosmic conflagration is not restricted to Jewish thought. Belief that the world undergoes a cycle of destruction, first by water and then by fire, goes back at least to Babylonian mythology and occurs in some strains of Greek philosophy (see Bauckham 1983, 301; Fornberg 1977, 66-67). The Stoics also envisioned a conflagration of the cosmos and a periodic purification of the universe by fire *(ekpyrōsis)*. Once the contamination is burned away, the universe is reconfigured in a pristine state (e.g., Seneca *Quaest. nat.* 3.28-29; Plutarch, *Moralia* 1067a. See also Justin *Apol.* 1.120.1; Origen, *Contr. Cels.* 4.11-13).

Undoubtedly, our author was affected by Jewish apocalyptic thinking, either directly or through the filter of early Christian teaching, but he also likely recognized some affinity between his beliefs and the Stoic idea of *ekpyrōsis*. Nevertheless, he also displays significant differences from both those cosmological constructions. For example, he does not believe that cyclical patterns of return govern the world. The present is analogous to the past, but does not recapitulate it. Second, the author is not interested in cosmology *per se*, but in proving that there is a future judgment for human sin. The elements of apocalyptic thought and of Stoic cosmology were simply used to convey the idea of universal divine judgment, not to propose a theory of cosmology. The structure of verse 7, which emphasizes the judgment motif, confirms this focus. The thought of the second half of the verse parallels the first:

7a: The present heavens and earth are reserved for fire.
7b: They are kept until the Day of Judgment and destruction of the godless.

The dramatic conclusion of the verse shows that the author's major concern is not cosmic annihilation, but the ultimate judgment and punishment of the ungodly.

The author's word choices further emphasize judgment. Elsewhere in the letter he refers to the second coming as "the day of the Lord" (3:10) or "the day of God" (3:12), but here he prefers "the day of judgment." As in 2:4, 9, he uses the verb *tereō* ("to keep") to remind the readers that the world is in the dock awaiting God's purposive judgment of the disobedient (2:4) and "unrighteous" (2:9).

◊ ◊ ◊ ◊

Verses 5-6 stress that God's creative word is neither static nor finished. God's past actions prefigure other future actions, but, more importantly, God's freedom to act is not bound by human understandings. God's interaction with the world reveals his desires for the present, but humans make a fatal error when they insist on accepting God as Creator while ignoring the reality of God as Judge. When human beings deliberately overlook the fact of God's past judgments, they ignore the reasons for those judgments and so invite their own destruction. In verse 7, the author describes the catastrophe in store for those who refuse to heed God's actions and will.

This passage is "perhaps the most difficult of several passages in 2 Peter which pose serious hermeneutical difficulties for the modern reader" (Bauckham 1983, 302). The author's cosmology, especially the idea of a cosmic conflagration for purposes of divine judgment, is foreign to late-modern Western thinking. Nevertheless, while his imagery must be interpreted, the author's ideas about moral accountability and ultimate responsibility before God pose an important challenge to contemporary believers. Believing in God as Creator has moral consequences, because God's commitment to the creation means that God will ultimately eliminate those who harm it (3:12-13). Thus, those who believe in a Creator God, one who is faithful to the creation, must display this same commitment to integrity and fidelity in their own lives.

Second Reply (3:8-10)

The author now attempts to answer the problem posed by the "non-occurrence" of the second coming. The scoffers objected that the "ultimate" event had not occurred either in the promised time frame or in the time since the "death of the fathers." They argued further that this "non-occurrence" was sufficient to discount belief in the second coming and therefore denied that there would be a final reckoning for human beings. While the author grants that the Parousia has not yet occurred, he does not accept that it will not occur. He interprets the "non-occurrence" as only a *delay* of the second coming and, in fact, argues that the delay is divinely motivated. Thus, the non-occurrence of the second coming is not evidence of God's inability or apathy toward the creation, but an indication of God's intention that all humanity enter "into the eternal kingdom."

The author's argument begins with an admonition "not to ignore this one fact," repeating the language of verse 5. In contrast to the scoffers who ignore the evidence of history and the activity of God in the creation (i.e., "the word of God," v. 5), the "beloved" audience should realize that human conceptions of time are not applicable to God. Only God's perspective is sufficient to interpret elapsed time, as the author's claim (based on Ps 90:4) that "with the Lord one day is like a thousand years and a thousand years are like one day" makes evident. The psalm stresses that God has sovereignty over the entire universe, including the passage and measure of time itself. It also contrasts God's eternal nature with human transience; human life is too brief to comprehend the scope and purpose of God's plans. The author applies the psalmist's ideas to the issue of the non-occurrence of the second coming and God's plan for its delay.

The non-occurrence occasioned significant confusion for early believers, and in verse 9 the author cautions his readers not to consider it as an indication of God's lack of concern or an inability to interact with creation. The author maintains that the Lord "is not slow about his promise, as some think of slowness." This phrase may echo Hab 2:3, which Jewish interpreters often used to explain God's apparent delay in acting on Israel's behalf (so Bauckham 1983, 310). Faithfulness to God requires a willingness to wait on God's promised action, especially when all visible evidence points in a contrary direction.

The problem posed by divine delay was not restricted to Jewish thought, but also permeated Greek speculation about the divine nature. Plutarch's *The Delay of Divine Judgment*, for example, contains a dialogue about "the slowness of God" in dealing with the wicked. One of his conversationalists views this "slowness" as a telling argument against the Deity's intervention in human affairs (*Mor.* 548C, 549B). In response, the other conversationalist notes that God knows the best moment to act (*Mor.* 551C); any apparent delay is only a demonstration of God's gentleness and magnanimity. Our author's arguments follow a similar line of reasoning.

The author also argues that a delay does not mean that the promise of Christ's return has been annulled. God does not delay the second coming because of slowness, but from divine patience. Biblical writers repeatedly stress God's forbearance, especially in regard to the divine response to human sin and disobedience (Exod 34:6; Ps 86:15; Jonah 4:2; Rom 2:4, 9:22; 1 Peter 3:20). As those texts demonstrate, God's forbearance is an element of divine mercy, which, in the interim between human disobedience and divine retribution, provides opportunity for humans to repent and renew their commitments to God.

Jewish and Christian writers often connected God's patience with eschatological beliefs, including the appearance of "the day of the Lord" (Joel 2:11-13; *1 Enoch* 60:5; Acts 17:30-31). The author follows that practice here, but he also holds that the time for repentance will cease one day and a time of judgment will begin. Because the day of the Lord is the final moment of history, God delays it as long as possible, providing through his compassion one last chance to repent. God delays that day because God does not want "any to perish, but all to come to repentance."

The words "any" and "all" stand in a complementary relationship. God's desire is that no one should perish. However, since the author has already noted that the pre-flood world perished (3:6; *apōleto*), and he affirms that the current world will undergo destruction (*apōleias*; 3:7), it is clear that "all" cannot mean every human being. He therefore does not think God's compassion will result in universal repentance. Hence, his use of "all" in this verse must refer to members of the audience who have repented or will soon repent. This sense is consistent with the preceding thought that the Lord is patient "with you."

In verse 10, the author stresses that although God delays the judgment, most assuredly it will occur. He places the verb "will come" at the beginning of the Greek sentence to emphasize this certainty. Moreover, the day will arrive suddenly, unexpected and surprising like the break-in of a thief (see Matt 24:43; 1 Thess 5:2; Rev 3:3, 16:15). The "day of the Lord" is equivalent to the "day of Judgment and destruction" (3:6, 12). The roots of the image are found in the prophetic tradition, which spoke of the time when Yahweh would execute judgment, punishing the unrighteous and rewarding the righteous (e.g., Isa 13:9, Joel 1:15, Amos 5:18-20).

The next part of the verse expands the idea of suddenness and describes the effects of the judgment on the physical and social orders. The imagery returns to the initial argument about destruction (3:6) and prefigures the conflagration of the creation (3:11-12). Three poetic clauses describe the radical changes to the three different spheres of the created world (the heavens, the stars and planets, and the earth). All the clauses portray the same catastrophic event, but each presents a different facet. The sequential relationship of the images and their rapid succession underscore the magnitude of God's judgment as well as the totality of the change God will bring about. The day of the Lord brings nothing less than a new creation (3:13), so the old order and societal make-up will undergo a complete and total alteration.

When the day of the Lord dawns, "the heavens will pass away with a loud noise." The onomatopoetic adverb *roizēdon* ("loud noise") often was used to describe a whizzing, hissing, or crackling noise (BDAG, 907). Here it evokes a sudden explosion culminating in a roaring fire through which "the elements" *(stoicheia)* are dissolved.

In many contexts *stoicheia* refers to the basic elements from which all nature is composed (fire, water, earth, and air), in others to spiritual powers (Gal 4:3, Col 2:8), or astral bodies like the Sun, moon, and stars. Since the author has distinguished three spheres of the final cataclysm, and since he has just referred to the dissolution of the heavens (v. 10*b*) and will next speak of the conflagration of the earth (v. 10*d*), the present clause (v. 10*c*) likely refers only to the intermediate sphere. This means that *stoicheia* should be understood as a reference to the incineration of the celestial bodies located in the middle sphere (also Isa 13:10, Ezek 32:7-8, Mark 13:24-27, Rev 6:13).

The final clause of verse 10 is difficult to interpret because of the verb *heurethēsetai* ("will be found"). The textual variants and proposed textual emendations highlight the difficulty. The best textual witnesses read "will be found" *(heurethēsetai),* but this reading produces little sense in relation to the two preceding clauses. As a result, interpreters adopt one of three alternative strategies: (1) Emend the reading so that a sense of destruction is conveyed. Some commentators substitute a word like "burning" or "fire" in place of "will be found." Others suggest that the word *ouk* ("not") was dropped from later copies of the letter and should therefore be reinserted into the "original" text (so Bigg 1961, 213; Fornberg 1977, 76). The simplicity of this emendation and the clarity it brings make it a genuine option: "the earth and everything that is done on it will not be found." (2) Adopt one of the textual variants found in the ancient manuscripts. Unfortunately, none of these variants has strong attestation; all of them were secondary attempts to solve the problem posed by *heurethēsetai.* (3) Accept *heurethēsetai* as the correct reading and provide alternative translations of the term. Hence, some commentators suggest that the verb refers to God discovering (i.e., judging) the earth and its works. This choice appears to be the preference of the NRSV translators ("will be disclosed"). Although this option breaks with the previous images to a degree, it does fit well with verse 14, where the related verb *heurethēnai* is also used.

◊ ◊ ◊ ◊

The author of 2 Peter was not the first interpreter to explain temporal anomalies or supply chronological explanations by applying the formula found in Ps 90:4. Jewish interpreters and later Christian exegetes also used this psalm to establish extended timelines. Typically, they would quote a biblical text that included the word "day," and then perform a "sacred mathematics" by substituting one thousand years for each occurrence of that word (Elliott 1982, 155). Barnabas, for example, reinterprets Gen 1:1–2:3 in order to "demonstrate" that God's resting on the *sixth day* actually means "that in *six thousand years* the Lord shall bring all things to an end; for the day with him signifies a thousand years" (*Barn.* 15:4-5). This interpretive technique was also used to explain the length of Adam's life, to compute the length of the messianic reign, and to calculate the end of the world (see Neyrey 1993, 238; Bauckham 1983, 306).

Our author, however, is the first exegete to turn the usual interpretive practice in on itself. Rather than use the psalm to show that God's actions can be predicted, he uses this "mathematical technique" to prove that a timeline for God's actions cannot be determined by humans because God's time frames and courses of action are incomprehensible to them. Hence, the "delay" of the second coming only appears as a delay from the intrinsically limited human perspective. From the divine perspective, the second coming will occur exactly when planned.

In verse 9, the author explains that "the delay" provides time for God's ultimate purpose and desire for all creation to be realized. God's reconciliation and redemption of humanity requires a return to God and a commitment to live righteously (Isa 49:17-19, Hosea 14:1-7, Rom 6:8-14). Believers must continue in their commitments while they await the consummation of the universe. In verse 10, the author reminds the readers that ultimately the universe will be judged and the true nature of every element and action revealed. Thus they must now live unblemished lives, waiting for the promised return of Christ.

Throughout the epistle (and especially in 3:5-10), the author has insisted that a final judgment of human behavior will occur. In 3:10, as in 3:7, the dissolution of the heavens and the earth leaves the behavior of the ungodly (and godly, v. 14) exposed to the sight of the Lord. The author has used cosmological imagery, but his chief concern has been human accountability.

Eschatological Exhortations (3:11-16)

Having established that there will be a future judgment and that the present world will pass away, the author informs the audience that their conduct must anticipate the final judgment. New Testament letters conventionally include a hortatory section motivated by eschatological convictions (e.g., Rom 12:3-21; Gal 5:5-22, 6:7-10; Eph 5:3-20; 1 Thess 5:11; 1 Pet 5:1-10). Parenesis of this sort is also found in "farewell testaments" such as *1 Enoch* 91:3-19, *Jub.* 36:3-11, and *2 Apoc Bar* 84-85.

The author considers the present world corrupt (1:4) and inhospitable to the righteous (2:9-10). He also knows that the rescue of believers from the present age and the judgment to come is God's ultimate goal. He further holds that believers are destined for "entry into the eternal kingdom" (1:11). As a result, their lives should even now reflect the character of that realm (1:5-8). The exhortation of verses 11-16 underscores this.

The thought is divided into two parts: verses 11-13 and verses 14-16. The first section explicates the moral implications of the preceding arguments and the second section reminds the readers of the perils of ignoring the moral requirements of eschatological existence.

◊ ◊ ◊ ◊

A Question about Eschatological Existence (3:11-13)

In verse 7 the author asserted that, "the present heavens and earth" are under indictment, "kept for judgment," and in verse 10 he declared that, "the present creation will pass away." In verse 11 he presents a corollary of this argument. "Since all these things" (i.e., the present heaven and earth) "are to be dissolved in this way," Christians should await the end by living lives of "holiness and godliness." Believers' lives must remain true to the past while also being future oriented. Believers "are waiting for" and "hastening" the "coming of the day of God" (v. 12). The first verb, "awaiting," is used three times in verses 12-14, creating one thought unit. Verses 12 and 13 are a parallel pair, and verses 14-15a serve as a conclusion to the ethic proposed in them. Since the believers know that this world will be dissolved *(lyomenōn)* (v. 11), they should wait for ("orient themselves toward," *prosdokōntas)* the coming day of God (v. 12). Because they know that the present heavens will be dissolved *(lythēsontai)* (v. 12), they must wait for ("anticipate," *prosdokōmen)* the new heavens and earth (v. 13).

◊ ◊ ◊ ◊

The participle "dissolved" that modifies "these things" is in the present tense and, while the NRSV's "are to be dissolved" is acceptable since in Koine Greek, present tense participles often take future meanings (e.g., *kolazomenous* "under punishment," 2:9), a better translation is, "are being dissolved." The present tense indicates that the dissolution of creation was already under way and, therefore, that the coming day of the Lord could not be far off. The verb form intensifies the author's exhortations because it emphasizes that God is, even now, altering the world in preparation for the day of judgment (so Kelly 1981, 366 and Mayor 1965, 161).

The term "what sort of" in verse 11 can have a positive or negative nuance (e.g., Matt 8:27, Mark 13:1, 1 John 3:1). When positive, as here, it qualifies a life of moral excellence and integrity, and "hints that great things are expected of the readers" (Kelly 1981, 366-367). The plural forms of the nouns "holiness and godliness" underscore that many kinds of godliness characterize the Christian life. Godliness and holiness are not simply parts of the Christian life, but apply to every facet and mode of the believer's conduct.

Exhortations to live expecting the day of the Lord are common in the New Testament (Matt 24:45-51; Mark 13:28-31; Luke 21:29-36; 1 Thess 5:6). Its location between remembrance of God's past actions in Christ and God's future actions through Christ defines Christian existence. The author offers similar instruction, but in verse 12, he adds an idea not typically found in the New Testament: the repentant actions of the believers can "hasten" the day of judgment (Acts 3:19-20 is the one parallel). Later first-century Christian texts such as *2 Clem* 12:6, *Herm. Sim* 10:4:4, and *Barn.* 4:3 develop the notion of "a hastened day." A number of Jewish texts also refer to God's hastening the day of judgment (Isa 60:22*b*, *Sir* 36:8, *2 Esdras* 4:33-39, *2 Apoc. Bar.* 20:1-2). A classic example from the Talmud reminds Jews that the Messiah will appear if Israel can repent only for one day (*b. San* 97*b*, 98*a*, *b*; *Yoma* 86*b*; see Bauckham 1983, 325; Kelly 1981, 367; and Vögtle 1994, 241 for discussions of the rabbinic parallels).

The expression "the coming day of God" is unusual. Elsewhere in the New Testament the word *Parousia* ("coming") has a personal subject, but here the reference is to a coming day. Moreover, New Testament writers usually speak of "the Day of the Lord" (Acts 2:20, 1 Cor 1:8, 5:5, 2 Cor 1:14, 1 Thess 5:2), "not the day of God." Despite the variations, the author is referring to the same final events. The fire imagery, the dissolution of the heavens, and the burning of the elements (v. 10) are repeated, preparing for the culminating image of "new creation" (v. 13).

The author does make two noteworthy changes from the wording of verse 10. First, he states that the heavens will be kindled "because of" the coming day. God will cause the burning of the heavens; they are not ignited as the result of a natural cyclic process like that proposed in Stoic thought (so also Kelly 1981, 367-368). Second, the *stoicheia* ("elements") are said to melt with fire. This is fundamentally a poetic/stylistic change, but the verb choice is significant. The verb *tēkeothai* ("to melt") occurs only here in the New Testament, but in Isa 34:4 (LXX v. l.) and Mic 1:4 it refers to the eschatological day of judgment when the Lord's wrath is unleashed against transgressors (see also *T. Levi* 4:1, *1 Enoch* 1:6, *2 Clem* 16:3).

Hence the verb itself signals the eschatological trauma on the horizon.

The pattern established in verses 5-7 (creation, judgment, recreation) now recurs. God's ultimate act is not destruction but recreation, and the audience must remember this final goal while they live toward the future. The author concludes, "we wait" not only expecting a day of judgment (v. 12), but simultaneously anticipating "new heavens and a new earth." The term "promise" recalls God's promise of salvation from this corrupt world (1:4). Such formulations were typically part of Jewish apocalyptic beliefs (e.g., *1 Enoch* 45:4-5; 72:1; *Sib. Or.* 5:212) that were adopted by early Christians (Matt 19:28, Rom 8:19-22, Rev 21:1). The author probably had in mind the promises of new creation mentioned in Isa 65:17 ("For I am about to create a new heavens and a new earth;" see also Isa 66:22), but the reference is too vague to indicate a specific source.

The actions of God, especially those of the future, should shape the present existence of God's people. Though "righteousness" is a characteristic of the new creation (e.g., Isa 32:16-18, 41:3; *1 Enoch* 45:4-6; *2 Enoch* 65:8), it is a necessary aspect of human existence before God even now. Unlike the pre-flood world where the righteous ones were not at home (2:5), or the age of Sodom and Gomorrah where the righteous suffered (2:7-8), in the new creation righteousness will be the norm. Thus, those who wish to enter "the eternal kingdom" and dwell there must act righteously as they wait for the new world to dawn (3:10).

When that day will dawn is determined by God, but it is also affected by human behavior. These verses are thus a corollary to 3:9: God delays the day of judgment because of a desire that all "come to repentance." Here the author stresses the obverse point: the repentant behavior of Christians, characterized by lives of "holiness and godliness," "hastens" the "coming day of God." Simply put, as more repent, the day draws closer.

The Question of Eschatological Existence Answered (3:14-15a)

Verses 11-13 posed a question about present eschatological existence, and verses 14-15*a* provide its answer. For the author, "waiting" is not a passive state but an active engagement in "godliness," which the exhortative "therefore" makes clear. The new world of righteousness requires righteous, holy living now. Three elements characterize such a life: "striving to be found at peace," living "without spot or blemish," and regarding "the patience of the Lord as salvation."

◊ ◊ ◊ ◊

Verse 14 reiterates the thought of verses 11-13 and reminds the readers of the letter's opening admonition: "Therefore *(dio)*, brothers and sisters *(agapētoi)*, be all the more eager *(spoudasate)* to confirm your call and election, for if you do this you will never stumble" (1:10). The author repeats the terms of the earlier verse *(dio, agapētoi, spoudasate)* but substitutes the phrase "to be found by him at peace, without spot or blemish" for the confirmation of their call and the promise that they will not stumble.

In contrast to the "false teachers" who were labeled "blots and blemishes" (2:13), the audience should strive "to be found by him (God) at peace, without spot or blemish." Originally, the expression "without spot or blemish" described animals acceptable for sacrificing to God (Lev 1:3, 3:1; see also comments on Jude 24), but eventually is was employed metaphorically for human moral purity. It appears frequently in this sense in the New Testament, especially with regard to the expected state of the Church at the second coming (Eph 1:4, 5:27; Phil 1:10; Col 1:22).

With a reverential circumlocution for God's actions the author exhorts the readers "to be found by him" in this state of moral purity. The phrase refers to the moment of judgment when people are deemed acceptable or unacceptable by God. This expression is equivalent to being "at peace," which refers not to a state of inner comfort, but to a reconciled existence with God (see 1:2

and the comment on Jude 2). The idea repeats that of 3:10: "the earth and all its works will be found" *(heurethēsetai)* (by God). Ungodly scoffers will be destroyed in that day (3:7), but faithful believers will "be found" by Christ at his return, because they will be discovered in right relationship with God, provided they live in "holiness" and "godliness."

Verse 15*a* presents another contrast between the audience and the scoffers. The scoffers consider the delay of the second coming as "slowness" or as evidence of God's inability to act (3:9). The audience, however, is to recognize the Lord's patience (3:9) as an opportunity for repentance and salvation.

Accepting Paul's Teaching on Eschatological Existence (3:15b-16)

The reference to Paul's letters in verse 15*b* continues the author's argument that the teaching about the future judgment is part of God's revelation. He has already noted that the apostles (1:16-18), the prophets (1:19-21), and scripture (3:13) attest to its reality; now Paul's letters are added to the list of inspired evidence.

Since it is likely that the opposition used Paul's letters to support their teaching about the future (see below on 3:16), the author now counters their strategy and himself enrolls Paul as an ally reclaiming his letters as evidence for the reality of a future judgment. The reference "to the wisdom given to Paul" links the apostle's teaching with the other established, fundamental sources of the gospel message (1:19-21). As a result, Paul's letters are removed from the opponents' arsenal and placed in the author's expanding pool of evidence against them.

◊ ◊ ◊ ◊

The author refers to Paul as "our beloved brother," which links him with the "beloved" audience (3:1, 8, 14). The term *adelphos* ("brother") often was used in the technical sense of a co-worker for the Lord (2 Cor 2:13, Phil 2:25, 1 Pet 5:12, Eph 6:21, Col 4:7). In combination, "our" and "brother" suggest that our author regards Paul as a fellow apostle. Thus, his letters carry the same authority as the author's apostolic teaching.

This reference to Paul's letters, especially those purported to have been written to the author's church, bear on the letter's audience and date of composition (see Introduction). Two pertinent questions concerning the sense of verses 15b-16 arise in this regard: (1) How does the phrase "according to the wisdom given to him" relate to the content of Paul's letters? and (2) Does the phrase "wrote to you" indicate that Paul wrote specifically to the author's audience, or does it mean that the Pauline correspondence was generally available throughout the Christian church? An answer depends on how one interprets the phrase "as in all his epistles" (v. 16).

The participle *dotheisan* ("given") has a central importance in this verse. *Dotheisan* is a "divine" passive: God has supplied the wisdom Paul has received (1 Cor 2:6-13; Gal 2:9). In this regard Paul's letters (and Paul) are functionally equivalent to "the prophecy of scripture" and its interpreter (1:20-21), all conveying truth supplied by God. In a similar argument, Clement reminds the Corinthians that Paul wrote "under the influence of the Spirit" in order to stress the authority of Paul's letters (*1 Clem* 47:10). Accordingly, he maintains that the church should heed Paul's admonitions because they originated with God. Our author's phrase, "the wisdom given to him" has the same sense. Paul was not relaying his opinions when he wrote about how Christians should live as they await the second coming; his writing was the result of divine revelation.

When the author states that Paul speaks "of this" in all his letters (v. 16), he is referring to ethical conduct in light of the Lord's return (contra Mayor 1965, 154-165). The author's steadfast concern with the relationship of eschatology and morality remains his focus here. As a result, it is best to understand the expression "of this" to mean all of the eschatological conduct mentioned in verses 14-15 (see Bauckham 1983, 330; Kelly 1981, 371).

One other issue requires attention before turning to the last part of verse 16: to which letter(s) of Paul did the author refer?

Commentators propose that the letter can be identified either by a consideration of its destination or of its content. The first option requires a particular interpretation of 2 Pet 3:1 and its relationship to 1 Pet 1:1. If the writer is claiming that his audience also received 1 Peter (see comment on 3:1), then any of Paul's letters to Asia Minor are candidates. If 3:16 refers to a specific Pauline letter, then it likely would have been Galatians, Colossians, or Ephesians, since these letters contain exhortations based on the expectation of the second coming. The Corinthian letters and 1 Thessalonians also contain eschatological exhortations, but they are addressed to churches outside of the region to which 2 Peter would have been sent.

It may, however, not be necessary to select one (or more) of the Pauline letters as candidates. Since 2 Peter displays no direct use of or dependence on Pauline ideas or language, it is reasonable to think that the author has only a general sense of Paul's letters. Most likely, as the comments on verse 16 will show, he makes this remark because his opponents were appealing to, and misinterpreting, Paul's letters. If that is the case, almost any of Paul's letters would qualify as the referent. In the end, the author's reference to Paul's letters is for rhetorical effect. He wants to show that the letters of Paul are in line with the teaching he is presenting.

The phrase in verse 16 "in all his letters" implies the existence of a nascent Pauline collection, known to the author and the audience. It is likely that the author is referring not to a formal, organized corpus, but to a small collection that was beginning to achieve authoritative status. However, as Kelly suggests, "we have no clue whether at this stage it comprised all, or only a selection of, the letters included in the New Testament" (Kelly 1981, 371).

The author's expansion of one letter (v. 15) to "all the letters" in verse 16 is not simply a benign repetition. Paul treated this matter not simply in the one letter known to the audience, but also in every letter he sent. If Paul repeatedly returned to these matters, then the author's own reminders must be taken most seriously.

In the final part of verse 16 the author grants that portions of Paul's letters are hard to understand *(dysnoēta)*. However, were the other teachers not "uninstructed and unstable," even these could be properly interpreted. The word *dysnoēta* does not occur anywhere else in biblical Greek and rarely in any ancient texts. In the few instances when it does appear, it refers to texts or oracles (Diogenes Laertius *Vit. Phil.* 9.13: Lucian *Alex.* 54) that are difficult to understand or interpret (LSJ, 459). The reference here must be to some passages in Paul that are complex or convoluted. Many of Paul's letters could qualify as "hard to understand," and it is impossible to determine exactly which passages the author might have had in mind.

Most generally, they were Pauline texts used by the opposition to instruct new believers. Perhaps the other teachers began with the idea that Paul's letters were difficult and claimed that only with their guidance could the congregation understand them. If so, two categories suggest themselves: passages that deal with the second coming (e.g., Rom 13:11-12, 1 Cor 15:51-56, 1 Thess 4:5) and those that speak of freedom from sin (e.g., Rom 4:13-25, 8:1; 1 Cor 6:12; Gal 3:23-29). In the first case, the false teachers might have taken issue with Paul's statements concerning the second coming. In the second case, the opponents, "who promise freedom," would have used his statements about release from the bondage of sin or the rule of law to support their position that Christians were no longer constrained by external ethic or moral codes.

The author refers to the opponents' interpretation as "twisting" *(streblousin)* Paul's words. This verb (only here in the New Testament) originally referred to a twisting or wrenching motion, like wringing a wet garment. Here it is applied metaphorically to the manipulation of texts to force from them ideas never intended by their original author.

The author's habit of pairing synonymous terms is evident again in his condemnation of those who twist Paul's texts. They are "ignorant and unstable" *(amatheis kai astēriktoi)*. The first term, *amatheis* (only here in the New Testament), refers not simply to ignorance but to the fact that someone is uninstructed, and hence lacks discernment. It is no wonder that they misinterpreted Paul; the false teachers did not possess the ability to interpret his material with any depth or understanding. The second term, *astēriktoi*, earlier described the unstable converts whom the false teachers had enticed into error (2:14), but here it depicts the false teachers themselves. They claim to be teachers, but they are untaught. They claim the wisdom of maturity, but they display the folly of the unstable.

The term "their own" recalls 1:20 where the author noted that, "no prophecy of scripture is a matter of *one's own* interpretation." But, contrary to the true prophets who spoke from God because they were moved by the Spirit (1:21) and, ironically, contrary to Paul (who was gifted by God with wisdom, 3:15), these teachers offer *their own* interpretations. The result is distortion and destruction. In the next verse, which deliberately plays on the words found here, the author warns his readers to "beware" lest you lose "your *own* stability." The readers will share the fate of the false teachers if they yield to the heretical teachings of the ignorant.

The false teachers apply their interpretations not only to Paul, but to the "other scriptures" as well. New Testament writers normally use the phrase "the scriptures" to refer to the Hebrew Scriptures (e.g., Matt 21:42, 22:29; John 2:22; 1 Cor 15:3; Jas 4:5), and that is likely the case here. By the late first century, however, some apostolic texts were also considered authoritative (e.g., 2 *Clem* 14:2), so the author could have meant apostolic writings as well (so Kelly 1981, 373). If so, it is his final denouncement of the opponents' error. Whereas he has shown that his teaching about future judgment finds backing in every conceivable source, his opponents warp prophecy (1:20), distort Paul (3:16), and misinterpret all other apostolic resources. Consequently, as he has maintained, their fate is sealed.

◊   ◊   ◊   ◊

The false teachers had used Paul's letters, interpreting them as evidence for their position. But their interpretations were simply the distorted, self-serving opinions of the uninformed. Thus, rather than producing truth or wisdom, the teachers bring about "their own destruction." Earlier, the author labeled them as "false teachers" who "in their greed exploit you with false words" and who "bring upon themselves swift destruction" (2:1, 3). Here he amplifies that point: they bring about their destruction not only by telling untruths but by manipulating the apostolic teaching to serve their own ends.

CONCLUSION AND DOXOLOGY (3:17-18)

Verses 17-18 resume the exhortation begun in verse 14, but they also constitute a conclusion to the letter as a whole. The term "beloved" and the catchword "stability" connect the admonitions of verses 17-18 to verses 14-16. The phrase "to grow in the grace and knowledge of Christ" (v. 18) describes actions that constitute "striving to be found by him at peace, without spot or blemish" (v. 14). In the same vein, the warning and the admonition apply not only to the immediate context, but also to the ethical practice of the Christian faith (1:3-11) and an awareness of the danger posed by the false teachers (2:1-3, 17-19).

◊ ◊ ◊ ◊

The emphatic pronoun in the phrase "you, therefore, beloved" (v. 17) differentiates the audience from the false teachers. In contrast to the "ignorant" and "unstable," who craft their own destruction (v. 16), the readers have been "forewarned" so that they can avoid being "carried away with the error of the lawless" and maintain their stability in the faith.

The participle "forewarned" recalls the fictional time frame of Peter's farewell testament. Not only had the audience been prepared by Paul's letters, but also by "Peter's" earlier prophetic warnings about false teachers (2:1-3; 3:3-4). Now it also has received Peter's last testament, delivered to remind them of his teachings and prepare them for the dangers that will arise after his death. Since they have received the teaching of both Peter and Paul, they should be prepared to resist false teachers and their false doctrine.

They are "to beware" or "guard against" the intrigue of the false teachers lest they be "carried away by/with the error of the lawless." The verb "carried away" is used with a similar sense in Gal 2:13 where Barnabas is said to have been "led astray" by hypocrisy. The phrase "the error of the lawless" repeats language used earlier to describe the pagan life (2:18), but here it refers to apostate activity or to false teaching. In this sentence the word "error" can have either a passive or active sense (see comment on Jude 11). It could be translated as "with the error of the lawless" (i.e., an error in doctrine, so the NRSV), or, if the active sense of the word is chosen, as actions that lead astray. In this case, the phrase would refer to the activity of the false teachers as well as to their teaching. The grammar is ambiguous, and a decision is difficult, but given the context and the author's continual references to knowledge, wisdom, and understanding in the previous section (3:15, 16, 18), it is reasonable to take the term as "error in doctrine."

Those who hold and advance erroneous doctrines are referred to as "lawless." In 2:7 the author used this term to describe the inhabitants of Sodom and to emphasize their disobedience and immorality. Moral laxity is probably implied here as well, in keeping with the author's efforts to connect false teaching and immorality. The term "lawless" links this exhortation antithetically with the preceding one, which called the audience to a life "without spot or blemish" (3:14).

The author warns the audience that it could "lose its own stability" if it does not guard against the inroads of the false teachers. The phrase "own stability" is deliberately used in contrast to the opposition who were described as the "unstable" who twist the scriptures "to their own destruction" (v. 16). The word *stērigmos* ("stability") is rare in ancient Greek and occurs only here in the New Testament (see 1:12 for comments on 2 Peter's use of this word-group). Its use creates a stark contrast between the faithful members of his community and the "unsteady souls" *(psychas astēriktous,* 2:14) who have followed the false teachers. The audience is already "established" *(estērigmenous)* in the truth (1:12), so they already possess a defense against the false teachers. They must maintain this defense by relying on the gospel message they have received, including belief in the second coming.

Verse 18 repeats the last admonition in a positive hortatory form. Not only should the readers guard against the false teachers, they should "grow" in grace and knowledge of the Lord. This verb typically was used for the organic growth of plants, but New Testament writers also employed it in metaphors for the believer's growth in knowledge (Col 1:10), righteousness (2 Cor 9:10), and faith (2 Cor 10:15), and that is its function here. The nouns "grace" and "knowledge" repeat language from the beginning of the letter (1:2) and thus create an *inclusio* between the letter's opening and ending. "Grace" should be understood separately from "the knowledge of Christ" and refers to the favor that God has shown (1:2, 3). In effect, the audience is called to grow in its experience of God's graciousness and to deepen its knowledge of Christ. The term for knowledge used here *(gnōsis)* is differentiated from the related word *(epignōsis)*, which denotes the foundational knowledge of God's actions in Christ (1:1). *Epignōsis* knowledge results in conversion (see comment on 1:2), but the *gnōsis* in verse 18 refers to a maturing knowledge. Throughout his letter the author has attempted to lead the audience from an early form of understanding to a deeper one, and now he calls them to continue enhancing their knowledge.

Most New Testament letters follow conventional epistolary practice and end with postscripts. Second Peter, however, does not have a postscript because a "last testament" would not contain final greetings or the mention of emissaries. The epistle ends, therefore, with a simple doxology, one of the most basic and unadorned in the New Testament. Only its peculiar reference to the "day of eternity" and the fact that it is addressed to Christ rather than God, mark it as unusual.

Doxologies addressed to Christ are rare in the New Testament (only here, Rev 1:5-6, and perhaps 2 Tim 4:18). Our author, however, has an elevated understanding of Christ's nature and function, and he ascribes to Christ attributes that other New Testament writers reserve for God (e.g., 1:1, 3, 17). The fact that the doxology is addressed to Christ is another example of this practice.

The time reference "both now and to the day of eternity" includes two unusual constructions: "both now and to" and "the day of eternity." The extremely rare phrasing "both now and to" (elsewhere only *1 Clem* 61:3 and *Mart. Pol.* 14:3) resembles Jude 25, a doxology which the author likely used as a model (see comment on Jude 25). The author has adopted Jude's reference to the present, dropped his reference to the past, and then re-emphasized the reference to the future by referring to the "day of eternity."

Most New Testament doxologies conclude with the phrase "forever and ever" (see Rom 16:27, Gal 1:5, Phil 4:20, 2 Tim 4:18). In 2 Peter, however, this expression has been replaced by the phrase "the day of eternity." This phrasing is almost unique in ancient literature, occurring elsewhere only in *Sir* 18:10— "Like a drop of water from the sea and a grain of sand so are a few years in the day of eternity." While the expression can be taken as a simple reference to eternity, it is likely that the author has used it to underscore the day on which eternity will be inaugurated, the day which dawns with Christ's *Parousia*. This final phrase thus emphasizes the day of the second coming one last time and ends the letter by stressing that the eschatological day truly will occur (3:10, 12). The doxology concludes with an affirmative Amen, "Let it be so."

◊ ◊ ◊ ◊

The conclusion to the letter is terse. The opposition has created a potential for crisis and disaster, but "Peter" has fore-warned his audience, and they must heed his admonitions. Though the truth of God's benevolence is real, and though they have been granted "knowledge" of that reality through God's actions in Christ, they must not abandon their allegiance. Second

Peter thus ends with a call to steadfastness. This exhortation is not a call to self-reliance, however, but to reliance on God's grace. The gospel is the announcement that God has supplied "everything needed for life and godliness" (1:1), but it also pronounces the responsibility "to conform to [God's] call and election" (1:10) by living a life of virtue (1:5). God desires a righteous life (3:11-12) and structures time so that all of creation may be redeemed (3:9). "Peter's" audience now knows these things, as do any readers of the letter, and they must heed his "testament" and its warnings by bringing their actions into line with their beliefs. Should they do so, their Amen will confirm their allegiance to God and their willingness to stand fast as God's people.

SELECT BIBLIOGRAPHY

BOTH CITED AND NOT CITED,
BUT EXCLUDING COMMENTARIES

Bauckham, Richard. 1980. "The Delay of the Parousia." *TynBul* 31:3-36.

———. 1988. "The Letter of Jude: An Account of Research." In *ANRW*, II. 25. 5, edited by W. Haase, 3791-3826. Berlin/New York: de Gruyter.

———. 1988. "2 Peter: An Account of Research." In *ANRW*, II. 25. 5, edited by W. Haase, 3713-3752. Berlin/New York: de Gruyter.

———. 1990. *Jude and the Relatives of Jesus*. Edinburgh: T&T Clark.

Boobyer, George Henry. 1958. "The Verbs in Jude 11." *NTS* 5:45-47.

Cavallin, H. C. C. 1979. "The False Teachers of 2 Peter as Pseudo-Prophets." *NovT* 21:263-270.

Charles, J. Daryl. 1990. " 'Those' and 'These': The Use of the OT in the Epistle of Jude." *JSNT* 38:109-124.

———. 1991a. "Jude's Use of Pseudepigraphical Source-Material as Part of a Literary Strategy." *NTS* 37:130-145.

———. 1991b. "Literary Artifice in the Epistle of Jude," *ZNW* 82:106-124.

———. 1993. *Literary Strategy in the Epistle of Jude*. Scranton, PA: University of Scranton Press.

———. 1994. "The Use of Traditional Material in the Epistle of Jude." *Bulletin of Biblical Research* 4:1-14.

———. 1997. *Virtue Amidst Vice: The Catalog of Virtues in 2 Peter 1*. JSNT Sup1 50. Sheffield, England: Sheffield Academic Press.

Charlesworth, James H. ed. 1983. *OTP*. Vol 1 *Apocalyptic Literature and Testaments*. New York: Doubleday.

Chester, A. and R. Martin. 1994. *The Theology of the Letters of James, Peter, and Jude. New Testament Theology*, edited by J. D. G. Dunn. Cambridge: Cambridge University Press.

Curran, John T. 1943. "The Teaching of 2 Peter 1.20: On the Interpretation of Prophecy." *TS* 4:347-368.

Danker, Frederick. W. 1978. "2 Peter 1: A Solemn Decree." *CBQ* 40: 64-82.

Desjardins, M. 1987. "The Portrayal of the Dissidents in 2 Peter and Jude: Does it Tell Us More about the 'Ungodly' than the 'Godly'?" *JSNT* 30:89-102.

Elliott, John H. 1969. "A Catholic Gospel: Reflections on 'Early Catholicism' in the New Testament." *CBQ* 31:213-223.

———. 1992. "Peter, Second Epistle of." *ABD* 5:282-287.

Ellis, E. Earle. 1978. "Prophecy and Hermeneutic in Jude," in *Prophecy and Hermeneutic in Early Christianity: New Testament Essays. WUNT* 18. Tübingen: Mohr-Siebeck. 221-236.

Farkasfalvy, Denis. 1985. "The Ecclesial Setting of Pseudepigraphy in Second Peter and Its Role in the Formation of the Canon." *SecCent* 5: 3-29.

Foerster, Werner. 1971. In *Theological Dictionary of the New Testament* 7, edited by G. Kittel and G. Friedrich, 1003-1012. Grand Rapids, MI: Eerdmans.

Fornberg, Tord. 1977. *An Early Church in a Pluralistic Society: A Study of 2 Peter.* ConBNT 9. Lund: C. W. K. Gleerup.

Greene, J. T. 1992. *Balaam and His Interpreters: A Hermeneutical History of the Balaam Tradition.* Atlanta: Scholars Press.

Harvey, A. E. 1990. "The Testament of Simeon Peter." In *A Tribute to Geza Vermes, Essays on Jewish and Christian Literature and History*, edited by Philip R. Davies and Richard T. White. JSOT*Sup.* Sheffield, England: Sheffield Academic Press. 268-285.

Hiebert, D. Edmond. 1985. "Selected Studies from Jude. Part 1: An Exposition of Jude 3-4." *BSac* 142:142-151.

———. 1985. "Selected Studies from Jude. Part 2: An Exposition of Jude 12-16. *BSac* 142:238-249.

———. 1985. Selected Studies from Jude: Part 3: An Exposition of Jude 17-23. *BSac* 142:355-366.

Holladay, Carl R. 1977. *Theios Anēr in Hellenistic Judaism: A Critique of the Use of This Category in New Testament Christology.* SBLDS 40. Missoula, MT: Scholars Press.

Johnson, Luke Timothy. 1999. *The Writings of the New Testament: An Interpretation.* Minneapolis: Fortress.

Joubert, S. 1995. "Persuasion in the Letter of Jude." *JSNT* 58:75-87.

Käsemann, Ernst. 1982. "An Apologia for Primitive Christian Eschatology." In *Essays on New Testament Themes*. Philadelphia: Fortress. 169-195.

Kee, Howard. 1972. "The Transfiguration in Mark: Epiphany or Apocalyptic Vision?" In *Understanding the Sacred Text*, edited by John Reumann, 137-152. Valley Forge: Judson Press.

Klijn, A. F. J. 1984. "Jude 5-7." In *The New Testament Age: Essays in Honor of Bo Reicke*, edited by William Weinrich, vol 3. 237-244. Macon, Georgia: Mercer University Press.

Kubo, Sakae. 1981. "Jude 22-23: Two-division Form or Three?" In *New Testament Textual Criticism: Its Significance for Exegesis*, edited by E. J. Epp and G. D. Fee, 239-253. Oxford: Clarendon Press.

Kurz, W. 1990. *Farewell Addresses in the New Testament*. Collegeville, MN: Liturgical Press.

Landon, C. 1996. *A Text-Critical Study of the Epistle of Jude*. JSNT*Sup* 135. Sheffield, England: Sheffield Academic Press.

Lyle, K. 1998. *Ethical Admonition in the Epistle of Jude*. Studies in Biblical Literature 4 New York: Peter Lang.

Neyrey, Jerome H. 1980a. "The Apologetic Use of the Transfiguration in 2 Peter 1:16-21." *CBQ* 42:504-509.

———. 1980b. "The Form and Background of the Polemic in 2 Peter." *JBL* 99:407-431.

Osburn, Carroll. 1972. "The Text of Jude 22-23." *ZNW* 63:139-144.

———. 1976-77. "The Christological Use of I Enoch i.9 in Jude 14, 15." *NTS* 23:333-341.

———. 1981. "The Text of Jude 5." *Bib* 62:107-115.

———. 1985. "I Enoch 80:2-8 (67:5-7) and Jude 12-13." *CBQ* 47:296-303.

Picirelli, Robert E. 1975. "The Meaning of 'Epignosis'." *EvQ* 47:85-93.

Rowston, D. J. 1974-75. "The Most Neglected Book in the Bible." *NTS* 21:554-563.

Schnelle, Udo. 1998. *The History and Theology of the New Testament Writings*, translated by M. E. Boring. Minneapolis: Fortress Press.

Snyder, G. F. 1977. "The *Tobspruch* in the New Testament." *NTS* 23:117-120.

Soards, Marion. 1988. "1 Peter, 2 Peter, and Jude as Evidence for a Petrine School." In *Aufsteig und Nierdergand der römischen Welt* II. 25/5, edited by W. Haase, 3226-49. Berlin: de Gruyter.

Starr, J. M. 2000. *Sharers in Divine Nature: 2 Peter 1:4 in its Hellenistic Context*. ConBNTS 33. Stockholm: Almqvist & Wiksell International.

Talbert, Charles. H. 1966. "II Peter and the Delay of the Parousia." *VC* 20:137-145.

Watson, Duane. 1988. *Invention, Arrangement, and Style: Rhetorical Criticism of Jude and 2 Peter*. SBLDS 104. Atlanta: Scholars Press.

Winter, Sarah. C. 1994. "Jude 22-23: A Note on the Text and Translation." *HTR* 87:215-222.

Wolthuis, T. R. 1987. "Jude and Jewish Traditions." *CTJ* 22:21-41.

COMMENTARIES (BOTH CITED AND NOT CITED)

Bauckham, Richard J. 1983. *Jude-2 Peter*, WBC 50, Waco: Word. The most extensive treatment of the letters in English, and indispensable for critical analysis of their content and argumentative structures.

Bigg, Charles. 1961. *A Critical and Exegetical Commentary on the Epistles of St. Peter and St. Jude*. ICC. Edinburgh: T & T. Clark. Written in a classic style, focusing on grammatical and lexical study. The reader should have a thorough knowledge of Greek.

Craddock, Fred. B. 1995. *First and Second Peter and Jude*. Louisville: Westminster John Knox. A readable commentary that discusses the highlights of the letters and their theological import for today; intended for use in sermon preparation or Bible study.

Cranfield, C. E. B. 1960 *1 & 2 Peter and Jude*. London: SCM Press. A brief commentary that focuses on fundamental phrases and major themes; intended for use in sermon preparation or Bible study.

Elliott, John H. 1982. *I-II Peter/Jude*, ACNT. Minneapolis: Augsburg Publishing House. Brief but useful treatments of the argumentative and theological flow of the letters, and also useful for situating the letters in their surrounding culture.

Frankemölle, Hubert. 1990. *1. Petrusbrief, 2. Petrusbrief, Judasbrief*. NECHTB. 2nd ed. Würzburg, Germany: Echter Verlag. A technical commentary based on the Greek text, intended for use in ecclesial settings. A new translation highlights the grammatical issues of the material. The letters are situated as polemics produced by a minority religion in order to define its social boundaries.

Fuchs, Eric, and P. Reymond. 1980. *La deuxième Épître de Saint Pierre; L'epître de Saint Jude*. CNT 13b. Neuchâtel, Switzerland:

Delachaux et Niestlé. Useful for its theological reflections and treatment of the major themes of the letters.

Green, M. 1968. *The Second General Epistle of Peter and the General Epistle of Jude*. TNTC. Grand Rapids: Eerdmans. A brief treatment that focuses on general themes and highlights.

Kelly, J. N. D. 1981. Reprint. *The Epistles of Peter and Jude*, HNTC. Grand Rapids: Baker Book House. Original edition, New York: Harper & Row. 1969. A very thorough treatment that moves through the fundamental thought units of the letters providing a balanced treatment of the interpretive problems.

Mayor, J. B. 1965. *The Epistle of St. Jude and the Second Epistle of St. Peter*. Grand Rapids: Baker. Interesting, if idiosyncratic. The comments focus on Greek grammar and philology and the excursuses provide interesting treatments of particular issues for interpretation.

Leaney, A. R. C. 1967. *The Letters of Peter and Jude*. Cambridge: Cambridge University Press. A brief commentary based on the NEB, which attempts to make scholarly findings available to the general public. Useful for determining the letters' main themes.

Neyrey, J. H. 1993. *2 Peter, Jude*. AB 37C. New York: Doubleday. This is a readable commentary that focuses on the social and rhetorical features of the letters. This format often reveals important aspects of the letter (e.g., the relationship to Epicurean thought), but occasionally it can be distracting and sometimes requires the author to pass over other interpretive features of the authors' arguments.

Perkins, Pheme. 1995. *First and Second Peter, James, and Jude*. IBC. Louisville: Westminster John Knox. A brief treatment that focuses on the general themes of the letters and their original settings. Like other volumes in this series it is intended for study and contemporary application.

Reicke, Bo. 1964. *The Epistles of James, Peter and Jude*. AB 37. New York: Doubleday. The original volume in the Anchor Bible series, subsequently replaced by Neyrey's commentary. Provides brief treatments of textual, historical, and linguistic features.

Richard, E. J. 2000. *Reading 1 Peter, Jude, and 2 Peter: A Literary and Theological Commentary*. Macon, GA: Smyth & Helwys. Approaches the letters as literary documents. It does a commendable job in covering the major themes of the letters while attending to specific issues of exegesis.

Schelkle, Karl Hermann. 1988. *Die Petrusbriefe, Der Judasbrief* HTKNT 13/2 6th ed. Freiburg: Herder. A detailed commentary;

argues for a Petrine tradition that shows connections between Jude and 2 Peter and in relation to Pauline thought.

Schrage, Wolfgang. 1973. *Die "katholischen" Briefe: Die Briefe des Jakobus, Petrus, Johannes und Judas*. NTD 10. 11th ed. Göttingen: Vandenhoeck & Ruprecht. A thorough and critical treatment, written at a scholarly level and intended for academic study of the material.

Sidebottom, E. M. 1967. *James, Jude and 2 Peter*. NCB London: Thomas Nelson. A very brief volume whose format allows it only to touch on interpretive issues. Nevertheless, interesting elements are included that help readers situate the letters in the cultural settings.

Vögtle, Anton. 1994. *Der Judasbrief, Der Zweite Petrusbrief*. EKKNT. Neukirchen: Neukirchener Verlag. A thorough and detailed analysis of the Greek text that is very helpful in critical study of exegetical issues. Reflects on the relationship of the opposition to Gnostic thought, and the question of who is authorized to interpret scripture.

Index